Advance Praise for *Painted Words*

"By sharing her paintings and poetry in *Painted Words*, Judy Endow provides rare insight into a person with autism, including her heightened sensory awareness, her need to establish predictability, her social needs, and much more. This captivating book tempts the reader to learn more about the uniqueness of autism and its neurological impact. Judy shares her experiences, asks thoughtful questions, and challenges the reader, by putting words and visuals to her early childhood. She provides her vision of the world, and her perspective will flood you with emotions and leave you looking through fresh lenses at those with autism. *Painted Words* is a wonderful gift to us so-called neurotypicals. We may very well feel like we are the ones that are lacking and, thus, not measuring up. Using her own words, I summarize Judy's contribution with this book by saying, 'The girl her mastery shows!'"—**Danette Schott**, M.A., executive editor, special-ism.com

"Judy Endow has long been one of my finest and clearest teachers when it comes to understanding autism. In *Painted Words*, Judy takes me into a new, deeper comprehension of her experience of autism using the mediums of poetry, prose and visual expression via her paintings. Her strong activist voice takes no prisoners, requiring me to examine how my own neurotypical arrogance can be a contraindicator in forming relationships with those in my life with autism. This strength is juxtaposed by the clarity of Judy's paintings, which provides both visual representation and softness, entering my consciousness in a manner completely different than the words that accompany and explain. Judy's ability to use her own experience to provide ideas and strategies for working with others is a treasure which she shares in each section of the book. *Painted Words* is a book that will appeal to autistics and neurotypicals alike, as we move forward to bridge the differences in how we experience the world to forge relationships and create better lives for those we love with autism."
—**Kate McGinnity**, M.S., educational consultant, and co-author of
Walk Awhile in My Autism and *Lights! Camera! Autism!*

"Judy Endow's *Painted Words* is a sensitive and beautiful portal into a life lived with autism. Through evocative paintings and poetry, Judy explores her own experiences and offers invaluable advice to parents, teachers and other professionals who work with people on the autism spectrum. This heartfelt book sparkles and glitters. Highly recommended."—**Jeanette Purkis**, author of *Finding a Different Kind of Normal: Misadventures with Asperger Syndrome*

"Judy Endow's *Painted Words* is an immersive, artful, and educational experience in understanding autism. Judy reveals her autistic neurology or 'operating system' by showing her way of perceiving, thinking, and learning. *Painted Words* is a step up from autism awareness. It is about understanding and accepting diverse minds."
—**Jill Jones**, filmmaker, currently researching and producing a documentary about autism and sensory perception (www.spectrumthefilm.com)

"Judy has brilliantly demonstrated her skill as a writer and an artist who proudly lives and loves autism. Her candid words and stunning art light up the spectrum as an example of the endless potential of all autistic people."—**Malcolm Mayfield**, specialist/consultant, founder of Autism STAR (Autism Spectrum Training, Advocacy and Recruitment), www.autism-star.com

"*Painted Words* takes the reader on an unforgettable journey far beyond written text—to a place where visual imagery dances with poetry to provide an intimate understanding of the world of an autistic. Judy Endow's powerful use of personal art work, poetry, and written text is a must read for every professional working with individuals on the spectrum."—**Ellen E. Eggen**, MS LPC ATR-BC, Art Therapist, Director of Planning and Operations, Common Threads Family Resource Center, Madison, Wisconsin

"What a wonderful book! In combining her talents in both writing and the visual arts, Judy Endow has given us an intimate look into her life with autism that is informative, engaging, beautiful, and thought-provoking. I cannot tell you how much I enjoyed this book."—**Peter Gerhardt**, Ed.D., Director of Education, Upper School for the McCarton School, and the Founding Chair of the Scientific Council for the Organization for Autism Research (OAR)

"Judy reveals her unique sensory experience in this generous and compassionate offering. Here, as always, her words provide keys to understanding the autism experience. Yet more remarkably, *Painted Words* reveals her experience through pristine and seminal art images that open the autism experience in ways that words cannot. The vivid colors and textures of her art invite us into her experience. Her ability to define crucial aspects of the autism experience is matched by precise suggestions to guide neurotypical connection and relationship with persons with autism. I hope *Painted Words* helps you listen and see with new eyes. Prepare to leave misguided conceptions of autism behind you."—**John B. Thomas**, M. Ed., educational consultant, and a principle author of *TEACCH Transition Assessment Profile (TTAP)*

Other Works by Judy Endow

The Hidden Curriculum of Getting and Keeping a Job: Navigating the social landscape of employment (AAPC Publishing 2013; co-authored with Brenda Smith Myles and Malcolm Mayfield)

Learning the Hidden Curriulum: The odyssey of one autistic adult (AAPC Publishing 2012)

Practical Solutions for Stabilizing Students With Classic Autism to Be Ready to Learn: Getting to go! (AAPC Publishing 2011)

2011 Hidden Curriculum One-A-Day Calendar for Older Adolescents and Adults: Items for understanding unstated rules in social situations (AAPC Publishing 2010)

2010 Hidden Curriculum One-A-Day Calendar for Older Adolescents and Adults: Items for understanding unstated rules in social situations (AAPC Publishing 2009)

Outsmarting Explosive Behavior: A visual system of support and intervention for individuals with autism spectrum disorders (AAPC Publishing 2009)

Paper Words: Discovering and living with my autism (AAPC Publishing 2009)

The Power of Words: How we talk about people with autism spectrum disorders matters! [DVD] (AAPC Publishing 2009)

Making Lemonade: Hints for autism's helpers (Cambridge Book Review Press 2006)

Cambridge Book Review Press
310 North Street
Cambridge, Wisconsin 53523
www.cbrpress.com
Editor: Bob Wake

Copyright © 2013
Judy Endow
www.judyendow.com

First printing, September 2013

ISBN 10: 0989402517
ISBN 13: 978-0-9894025-1-4

Painted Words
Aspects of Autism Translated

Judy Endow, MSW

Foreword by Ariane Zurcher, *Huffington Post* Blogger

My Dad passed away in January 2012.
This flower shows the bittersweet beauty of saying goodbye—
a tribute to a life well lived by Del Linders.

Delmar "Del" Linders,
May 19, 1931—January 2, 2012

Lavender Flower

Dedication 6
Foreword 10
Introduction 12

Growing Up

Chapter One: My World 19
    Sun Sparkles 20
    The World's Tail 26

Chapter Two: Myself 37
    Got the World By the Tail 38
    Sun Sparkle Girl 46
    Moon Sparkle Girl 48

Chapter Three: Other People 57
    Notice People 58
    Intrusion 66

Chapter Four: Accommodation 79
    People Accommodation 80
    Look Me in the Eye 86
    Beauty-Eyes Beholding 100
    People Inclusion 114
    People Break 118

Living

Chapter Five: Thinking 127
    Thinking Colors 128
    Inflexible Thinking 136
    Thought Waves 144

Chapter Six: Processing 151
    Blue-Green Leaves 152
    Blue-Green Leaves Variables 160
    Fractured Vision 168

Chapter Seven: Engaging 177
    Brown Paper Bags 178
    The Essence of People 184
    3 Panel People 192
    Connections 196
    Whispering Strength 198

Chapter Eight: Conclusion 203
    In Sidewalk Cracks 204

Epilogue 209
References 211
Artwork Chapter Index 213
Photo Credits 215

Foreword

"The aim of art is to represent not the outward appearance of things, but their inward significance." —Aristotle

I have never considered art in the way Judy Endow uses it in these pages. Judy is a writer, painter, sculptor, speaker, consultant, and autistic. *Painted Words: Aspects of Autism Translated* is so much more than an explanation or description of her neurology. It is a piece of art. Her written words, paintings and sculpture are woven together to create a depth of meaning that could not be accomplished each on their own. Judy describes how she comes to understand the meanings of words through the sound and movement of colors and then invites the reader to join her in doing so.

Her paintings and sculpture illustrate and emphasize her written words in an intricate and complimentary dance. Her brushstrokes—tiny waves of sound and color—become literal examples of what she is describing through prose. Judy not only shows us the inner beauty of her mind, she engages us, so we too can experience her words the way she does. In order to do this, the reader must dispense with any preconceived notions regarding autism, communication (either verbal or nonverbal), art and what it means to be autistic. We are invited to step inside a different neurology than our own. We are respectfully asked to question our assumptions, to consider autistic difference as neither less than nor superior, and to jump "into the crack between" together.

It may surprise the reader to learn that autism and being autistic is not what most believe. It may shock the reader to read of the joys and beauty that Judy experiences as an autistic person who has lived much of her life trying to understand our neurology as well as her own. Judy writes, "Some cannot see beyond the autistic scruffies and thus miss the blessings of individual autistic uniqueness." It is this "autistic uniqueness" that abounds. Gaze at one of her pictures, or at a piece of sculpture, and you will see a work of art, yet will miss so much. Read the words without the corresponding art, ignore the brushstrokes and color and you will not hear the beauty of her words. Read the words, *feel* them, *listen* to them while looking at the paintings and sculpture, *lean into the words* and you will come closer to understanding.

Judy describes and shows us how she perceives the world and by doing so shows all of us that what we view as "reality" is not the same for everyone. Her words and art are linked like conjoined twins who share a single heart. They cannot be separated. In order to fully understand, one must view them together. Judy encourages us to enter her reality, not because we pity those who are autistic or think it's the right thing to do, but because we, the entire human race—autistic and neurotypical—will benefit mutually from having done so.

Judy once posed the question, "What do you see when you look at these examples from my Brown Paper Bag series?" [178]

I have taken it upon myself to answer. I see beauty and effort. Colors bleed and change showing a fragile and vulnerable interior that is streaked with hints of rust and yellow. Color pushes itself up and out as though struggling to be heard and seen, some managing to spill out and over the edge in a show of strength and courage triumphant. The irregularly rippled exterior is shiny smooth and almost soft-looking, yet the essence of the piece is solid, almost impenetrable, except for the color. The warmth inside refuses to remain hidden. That softness, that vulnerability changes everything. It is both tender and strong. It is beauty. It is the moment when life becomes art.

Painted Words is Judy Endow's generous invitation to us to reflect on our humanness and to reject the misperceptions, misinformation and negative thinking regarding autism and autistic people. It is up to us to go the distance and accept her invitation to enter a reality that is beyond our wildest dreams.

Ariane Zurcher is a writer and award-winning artist, and the mother of a child with autism. Ariane lives in New York and blogs for *The Huffington Post*. Her work can also be read online at Emma's Hope Book (www.emmashopebook.com), and on her own website at www.arianezurcher.com.

Dear Reader,

Welcome! I am so glad you have my book in your hands. This is my tenth publication, but it is the first one in which I am sharing my art. This signifies a sharing of myself in a way and in a depth I have not yet done. It is scary, exciting and wondrous all at the same time. There are some things I want to tell you before you look at the art and read the words of this book.

My Experience of Autism

All human beings look out at the world through eyeglasses imposed upon them by their own neurology. Then, they assign meaning to the behavior of others according to the meaning that behavior would have were they themselves engaged in it. Most times the guess is correct, but sometimes—like when neurotypicals (NTs) are looking at autistics—the guess can be wrong.

This book is meant to give a view of the world from my vantage point—from inside my autism neurology. If you look at the art and read the words you will increase your success when you look at people with autism and make guesses about them.

People with autism share some similarities and even so, like my friend Stephen Shore says, "If you have seen one person with autism, you have seen one person with autism" (personal communication 2013). While it is true that the more you familiarize yourself with autistic people, the easier it becomes to understand autistic people, please keep in mind some autistics will have similarities to my experience of autism and others will not.

And just like no two human beings experience the world in exactly the same way, so it is true that no two autistic human beings experience the world in exactly the same way. Please learn what you can from my experience of the world, but do not ever assume my experience to be the experience of all autistics.

Unconventional Word Spacing

You will find some unconventional spacing as you read some of the poems associated with my paintings. This is because these words are a first translation of the paintings—a rudimentary rough draft, so to speak. The spaces between the words represent how long it takes for thinking colors to fluidly move in such a manner as to connect smoothly with the next thought.

Many times when the looks of these beginning words are changed I totally lose the looks of the painting. When this happens, there is no painting to further translate and hence no more words about that painting. It seems sort of crazy that changing spacing can be the same as completely deleting a poem, but it is so! I don't always like this, as in some cases I would rather have the words come more closely together so as to look more like traditional writing, but I have not been able to legislate this internally.

Check Marks

Check marks are followed by questions to ponder. Many times there are not immediate answers. The questions are posed to be helpful to you, the reader, if you want to consider how the aspect of autism being discussed might apply to you as you interact with, love, live with, teach or support your child, student, sibling, friend, parent or spouse on the spectrum. When helpful, please feel free to ponder the questions on your own or to discuss them with others.

Child and Student Word Usage

The words "child" and "student" are used interchangeably. Please know that "student" as used in this book includes all people because we are all learning and growing regardless of age. So while it may appear at first glance that this book is written for parents or teachers please know it is written for all people, and especially for autistic people.

My hope is that by sharing my own experience of the world those coming up behind me and autistics who are part of today's landscape will have something useful to ponder and perhaps become a bit more comfortable living inside their own skin while negotiating the neurotypical world all around us. I also hope autistics reading this book will be encouraged to share their own experience of the world.

Autistic and Person With Autism Word Usage

The words "autistic" and "person with autism" are used interchangeably. Some years back Kathie Snow was instrumental in raising awareness and usage of person first language (Snow, website accessed 2013). This language puts the person first and then the reference to his disability—thus, "person with autism." This way to use language invited us to change the way people with disabilities were talked about and thought about. It invited everyone to see people who had disabilities as people first.

Some people with autism did not like to be known this way. They felt that autism was an integral part of who they were as human beings and not simply an add-on. Just as they would not be described as a person with Jewishism, a person with femaleness, or a person with gayness, they did not want to be described as a person with autism. These friends want to be known for who they are as an autistic person.

And still to this day another group of my friends want to be referred to as persons with autism because they find it very important they be seen as people first. Many of these friends have expressions of autism such that when you see them coming you definitely SEE the autism and, therefore, it becomes really important to them that you see them for the person they are. Consequently, they prefer others to use person first language.

I have friends in both camps. Even though time is often spent debating which is the better way to use language when referring to people with an autism spectrum diagnosis I do not see this as a dichotomous polarized choice. I think both groups of my friends desire the very same thing. They want to be seen as the human being they in fact are! For some that means calling them a person with autism and for others it means referring to them as an autistic person. We all want our humanity to be recognized.

Kathie Snow's invitation to use person first language was an invitation to us all to come into a person first attitude. It is this person first attitude that unites the word usages of "person with autism" and "autistic." We all want to be included in the human race. And thus, I have honored all my friends by interchangeably using each one's preferred language throughout this book while at the same time recognizing it is the person first attitude that is the important construct. I invite you, as the reader, to use whatever language supports you in a person first attitude toward fellow human beings who happen to have an autism spectrum diagnosis.

Sincerely,
Judy

GROWING UP

Growing Up

Chapter One: My World

Sun Sparkles

Sun sparkles fill the sky today

Their force becomes too bold

Brightness, lightness way too much

My voice yells, "No, no, no!"

Sun Waves

Right Sun

Left Sun

An Aspect of My Autism

As a child I eventually came to love being outdoors, but I didn't always love it. In fact, I can recall the bright boldness of the sun being painful and of trying to duck away from it. By the time I was walking I knew this brightness was called the sun. Mostly I liked the sun sparkles, but some days I protested because the sun was so bright as to turn its sparkles into painful burning to my eyes. I became quite aware of which direction the pain from the bright sun came from at various times during the day (*Right Sun* and *Left Sun*). As a toddler I was tracking the sun and its amount of brightness so as to avoid the sensory impact of being hurt by this fireball as much as possible.

I noticed the sun made the air wavy (*Sun Waves*) right before it became too bright to tolerate. Because the wavy air was attractive to me, I did not immediately put it together that this was a warning of the too bright, eye-hurting sun that would quickly follow. Thus one minute I would be happily content sitting in the sandbox enjoying the sun waves I could see all around me, while the next minute protesting and hiding in the shadows of the garage to avoid the sun. I did not have language to use to explain this.

Considerations When Working With Others

- Sometimes children seem content one minute and then scream and tantrum the next minute. Often people are perplexed because it seems like nothing at all happened to cause the abrupt change in behavior. Even though that is your experience as a person looking on, remember your experience is rarely the experience of the autistic!

Atmospheric or environmental changes that seem so subtle as to not even be noticed by a neurotypical person (NT) are often experienced as a huge problem by an autistic person. Sometimes the magnitude of this difference is the difference between experiencing comfort and experiencing pain.

- ✓ Does your child go from appearing content to having a tantrum in no time at all?

- ✓ If yes, might there be a sensory component?

- It is more helpful to acknowledge that something is wrong when a child is in distress than to say nothing is the matter only because that is your perception or experience of the situation. To tell someone who is experiencing pain or discomfort that nothing is wrong undermines the development of a trusting relationship. When I find myself in these sorts of circumstances with students I simply say, "We will figure it out." This serves to align me with the student as a problem solver even when I do not yet understand the problem.

✓ What phrase might you use to align yourself with your child even when you do not understand the difficulty your child is experiencing?

The World's Tail

Predawn misty colors

Rise up from

The earth.

Predawn Tail

Come, morning sun

Awake new tail

It's almost time for birth!

Morning Tail

Wide Tail

Earth Tail

New morning suns

    Birth daytime tails—

    Each day a different one—

As last night's earthy mist

    Does kiss

    The new day's rising sun!

Earth-Tail Pink

Earth-Tail Purple

Water-Tail Pink

Water-Tail Purple

An Aspect of My Autism

I think in colors. My thinking colors have sound and movement. When I hear spoken words my neurology automatically goes for the match. When I was a girl I heard the saying, "I've got the world by the tail." Immediately, the matching pictures of my experience of the world popped up for me to see. I assigned the world tail words I heard to a literal tail meaning that enabled me to name the pictures that had popped up in my head (*Predawn Tail, Morning Tail, Wide Tail* and *Earth Tail*).

I assigned this new tail meaning to the interaction of the sunlight and misty water particles I could see rising up from the earth's surface whenever I was outside. For most of my life I thought this literally was the earth's tail. Moreover, I thought that people were somehow able to physically grab onto this tail and when they did so they indeed had the world by the tail!

I had always noticed the sun sparkles and the interaction of the sun sparkles with the earth mist. In fact, as a small child, they were often more salient to me than the people in my world. Most times I preferred them to people. I had often tried to touch these sparkles, but now I had a new mission. I wanted to actually catch this tail so I too might have the world by its tail (*Earth-Tail Pink, Earth-Tail Purple, Water-Tail Pink* and *Water-Tail Purple*)!

Considerations When Working With Others

- People with autism are often visual thinkers. It is not something we decide, but rather the way our brain handles information. We do not know when we are little that most other people think with words rather than with colors and pictures. This makes it difficult in school as delivery of information quickly becomes language-based as pictures drop away after the first few years. This dramatic change in materials in the United States occurs at the third grade level when text-based instruction becomes predominant.

For me it was hard to think about or understand ideas that were not concrete ideas. Basically, if my brain could not translate the words I heard into a concrete picture in a few seconds, as a young child I would not be able to pick up the meaning of the words being spoken. Even though I did not understand the meaning I was able to repeat the words. For example, when prompted I could repeat the teacher's instruction to use quiet voices even though I had no idea what the words meant because no picture popped up in my head to equal those words.

- ✓ Is your student a visual thinker?
- ✓ Do you use concrete language along with pictures as needed?

- When people with autism are able to recite your instructions or repeat an admonition and then do not follow the instruction or admonition do not assume willful noncompliance. Instead, check for comprehension. If the autistic is a visual thinker ask him to draw or show you what the instructions or rule looks like. If a visual thinker cannot do this, he likely does not comprehend the words you are speaking even though he may be able to repeat them quite accurately. Children with ASD have been shown to perform basically normal for age in word decoding, but lower than age expectation in reading comprehension (Minshew et al. 1994; Myles et al. 2002; Nation et al. 2006; Newman et al. 2007; Asberg et al. 2008; Asberg et al. 2010).
  - ✓ When your student's behavior has the appearance of willful noncompliance do you stop to ascertain comprehension before ascribing meaning to the behavior?
  - ✓ How will you evaluate your student's comprehension or lack of comprehension when his behavior looks like noncompliance?

- People with autism don't automatically pick up the meaning of idioms. However, they are able to learn the meanings of idioms by direct teaching. "I've got the world by the tail" is an example of an idiom. Sometimes a person with autism will automatically assign a literal meaning to an idiom and then assume everybody else shares that literal meaning because it makes sense to him! That is what I did in the above example using the idiom "I've got the world by the tail."
  - ✓ How will you teach the meanings of idioms and other kinds of assumed social understanding?
  - ✓ Do you check for shared meaning when it comes to idiom usage and understanding?

Growing Up

Chapter Two: Myself

Got the World By the Tail

Outside, time dawns bright for me

While Misty Earth is making

A bright New Tail that rises up

Then back to me for taking.

Summer-Tail Mist

Fall-Tail Mist

Seasons come and then come more

While tails my earth keeps making.

    Mist-Tails rise up from SNOW,

    And sometimes LAKE or EARTH—

Then sparkling back

    For me to catch

    Each misty tail breathtaking!

SNOW-Tail Mist

LAKE-Tail Mist

EARTH-Tail Mist

An Aspect of My Autism

People often described me as in my own world. They would say that I marched to the beat of a different drummer. Even though this is an idiom I suppose it was true in a sense because, after all, I was a child who tried for a very long time to literally catch the world's tail! This behavior of repeatedly trying to catch these sparkle tails probably did make me look different. It went on for several years and was an activity I very much enjoyed over the seasons of several years (*Summer-Tail Mist, Fall-Tail Mist, SNOW-Tail Mist, LAKE-Tail Mist* and *EARTH-Tail Mist*).

However, I was not in my own world. I was in the same world as all the others around me. I could not help it that other people could not see the details of the world such as the sun sparkles and the misty tails like I could see them, but that didn't mean our worlds were different. Instead our experience of the same world was different. My experience was much more robust because I had ever so much more to see than most people. I could also hear in a much more robust way than most people. In fact, my sensory experience of the world in general was always to a much higher refinement and greater impact than others.

If we used my experience as the norm then all the typical people would come up as very lacking. But we do not measure experience from the most to the least sensory quantity or quality perceived. Instead we measure according to what most of the people perceive and label as normal. Then any experience that does not fall into this normal range of experience is labeled abnormal and people with this abnormal experience are said to be lacking.

If the truth were told, whenever the neurotypical yardstick of normal is used to measure me I do not measure up to be very many inches (Endow 2009b). Because there is not a good way to measure the things that make me be me, those things go unmeasured. Instead I am measured by the yardstick of what makes you be you and I am found to be lacking.

Considerations When Working With Others

- Deficit-based language in the field of autism is used for diagnostic purposes. It is important because a diagnosis is what drives treatment. Early diagnosis and treatment have shown very good outcomes for youngsters with autism (Buron and Wolfberg 2008). The problem with deficit-based language comes when we take that deficit language out of the diagnostic arena and start using it to describe the humanity of a person with autism.

It is true that autistics are not like neurotypicals and that when measured we often land outside of the majority norm. Geniuses land outside of the majority norm, too. Landing outside of the norm does not equate to mean less than as a human being.

- ✓ Do you confine the use of deficit-based language to the diagnostic and treatment arena?

- ✓ How do you think about what is normal and what lies outside of normal?

- When autistics are treated as equal human beings positive relationships are more likely to develop. This is important because people with autism are generally able to learn new things and to access their highest level skills and abilities in the context of a positive relationship (Robledo and Donnellan 2008).

  - ✓ In your heart of hearts do you think of autistics as equal fellow human beings?

  - ✓ Do your relationships with autistics have a level of shared high regard for one another? What evidence do you have to support this?

- Don't allow yourself to write off autistics as "in their own world." In reality we are all in one shared world. Autistics tend to experience the world with a higher degree of sensory awareness and often interact with or guard against the impact of this different sort of experience by employing behaviors that can look different or unusual.

  Saying that someone is in their own world tends to give permission to disregard that person and to think of him as less than other human beings. When this happens everyone loses, including you.

  - ✓ If you talk about an autistic as "being in his own world" will you please stop?

Sun Sparkle Girl

Sun sparkles from the sky to me

A present to my soul

    Brightness, lightness now reigned in

    The girl her mastery shows!

Morning-Chirp Sun Girl

Night-Song Sun Girl

Cloud-Breath Sun Girl

Moon Sparkle Girl

When "Good-night, sun"

The moon does come

    Showing off night sparkles

    Dancing from the ground around

    Parading through earth's seasons.

Moon Sparkle Winter

Moon Sparkle Spring

Moon Sparkle Summer

Moon Sparkle Fall

An Aspect of My Autism

As I got older I saw over and over how light from the sun interacted with water particles rising from the ground and with water droplets in the air. This repeated experience became useful over time in that I learned the predictability of this occurrence. I also learned the effects that various factors (such as clouds, rain, air temperature, wind, etc.) had on impacting the interaction of sun brightness with air and ground moisture.

By the time I was old enough for kindergarten I had an extensive experiential knowledge of sun sparkles and thus could put myself into the picture of the sunlight in various circumstances (*Morning-Chirp Sun Girl, Night-Song Sun Girl,* and *Cloud-Breath Sun Girl*). Because I had figured out the predictability and pattern, I was able to attain mastery over a situation that once took me by surprise and caused unfavorable behavior reactions! With this newly found mastery I was now able to become part of the world around me, as literally seen in these paintings that now include the little girl of me.

I especially liked the moon sparkles. They were much less intense. I noticed the moon sparkles mostly by looking through the window as I lay on my bed at night. I learned the predictability of moon sparkles as one season gave way to another. I loved the predictable repeating pattern of sameness that I could see in so many ways as I watched the moon sparkles each night through my window (*Moon Sparkle Winter, Moon Sparkle Spring, Moon Sparkle Summer,* and *Moon Sparkle Fall*).

It was wonderful to have learned so many kinds of order to the world around me—an order I learned as I learned the pattern of sun sparkles and moon sparkles across the seasons. It is interesting that while I almost always saw moon sparkles from inside the house through the window, I do not ever remember noticing sun sparkles by looking out a window. I only remember the sun sparkles in the context of being outdoors.

Considerations When Working With Others

- I had many opportunities to gain mastery over the blinding sun sparkles due to the fact that children growing up in the 1950s played outdoors for many hours a day. Every day I interacted with what I saw by repeatedly trying to catch the sparkles and tails my eyes could see all around me. Looking back, I am so glad I grew up then and not now because back then children had much more imaginative play.

If I was a little girl growing up today and displayed the repetitive behaviors of catching sun sparkles and world tails it would likely be referred to as stimming and adults around me might try to stop the behavior. If that had happened I may never have sorted out the world by learning and using the various predictable patterns of atmospheric interaction between the elements of light and water. The behavioral stims of repeatedly trying to catch the sparkles and tails helped organize the world around me.

- ✓ Does your student have stims?

- ✓ Do you understand that stims can be organizing, relaxing and helpful?

- The neurology of a person with autism does not automatically organize the world outside their skin (Endow 2011). When we are able to organize the happenings in the world we usually do so differently than neurotypical people. For example, an autistic friend was tracking her way in a large convention center by noticing a small piece of paper trash on the floor at the place we were to take a turn. She had no realization that dropped trash may be removed by the time we needed to find our way back to where we started.

  We also thrive on predictability, sameness and routine (Endow 2009a). I organized my world in an unusual way using predictable atmospheric interactions of light and water. Most times we can help our children to organize more expediently by using a visual schedule that shows what will happen when throughout the day. Even so, do not discount their novel ways of organizing information if they are able to do so!

  - ✓ How does your child organize or make sense of the world?

  - ✓ How will you assist your child to organize or make sense of the world?

- Before I had my world organized I experienced lots of confusion, chaos and change each day. It was unsettling and anxiety provoking. It caused me to want to sit still and only look at books for long periods of time when I was indoors. For some children this perception of constant confusion, chaos and change in the world can precipitate meltdown behaviors.

  Oftentimes behaviors that don't work well in the world develop in response to the autistic perception of confusion, chaos and change. This is not intentional, planned or defiant behavior, but instead an unplanned reactive behavior.

  The way to provide support to prevent an autistic from a repeat of this felt experience of confusion, chaos and change is to provide a higher degree of predictability, sameness and routine in his world.

For example, if it is difficult for a child to stop his activity to get in the car to go somewhere, you could institute any number of supports such as using a visual timer to show ahead of time when it will be time to get ready and using the same "get ready" routine when you go somewhere in the car. One child's "get ready" routine involved (1) using the bathroom, (2) taking his already packed backpack to the car, and (3) putting on his seatbelt. He used this same transition routine every time he went somewhere in the car. After two weeks of learning and using this routine every day the meltdowns started fading. After two months the child stopped having meltdowns whenever it was time to go anywhere in the car. The transition from house to car had become predictable, was the same each time and had become the routine for leaving the house.

- ✓ If your child experiences confusion, chaos and change might he benefit from a stable, predictable routine of sameness to use at points of transition during his day?

- ✓ What practical elements will you include in a transition routine?

- I had an almost daily experience of being outdoors for many hours during the summer. I learned about the elements of sunshine, groundwater and mist droplets by observing how they interacted. It very much helped to have many of these same experiences every day.

Brenda Myles credits these multiple opportunities close together with the development of a critical mass (Myles, Endow, and Mayfield 2013). Once critical mass has developed for a particular experience, such as eating at McDonald's, that experience is no longer perceived as new and novel each time it occurs. Conscious attention no longer needs to be given to the routine ordinary details such as standing in line to order, getting condiments or sitting at a booth.

All new drivers develop critical mass. As they become familiar with aspects of driving, they no longer need to give conscious attention to staying in one lane, braking and accelerating. Individuals with autism often benefit from intentional support to develop critical mass.

- ✓ Do your children have enough tries or takes at the same experience to be able to learn the routine and come to enjoy the experience?

    EXAMPLE: If you want your daughter with autism to get used to eating at McDonald's she will need to go to McDonald's many times to enable her to track the routine, recognize the elements of sameness and make enough sense out of the experience for it to become predictable to her. Only then might she come to relax enough to enjoy eating at McDonald's.

Your daughter would likely learn this skill much more quickly if she were to go to McDonald's every day or at least several times a week while in the learning process than to go only once a month. Many times we do not give autistic children enough opportunities close enough together to enable their neurology to pick up the elements of predictability, sameness and routine in a situation so they are left with the once a month McDonald's experience of confusion, chaos and change for many years.

Growing Up

Chapter Three: Other People

Notice People

Notice people, important beings

Comprised of way too much

      Overpowering, powerful darks from earth

      Versus wondrous-air, sky-glorious stuff.

Sky Glory Blue

Sky Glory Diamonds

I pay no mind to powerful darks

When air colors beckon me

    Towards oneness with melodious movement

    Transcending my very being

Sky Glory Day

Sky Glory Moon

An Aspect of My Autism

When I started school I began noticing people who were not part of my family. Initially, I resented the intrusion they represented. The sparkles and world tails had my attention. I could not understand why people were trying to insert themselves where, in my estimation, they did not belong—into the predictability of my everyday awareness and interaction with the sparkles and tails all around me. At that time I perceived people as nothing but dark, dull bits of stuff that were impossible to systematically learn about because they had no salient-to-me predictability, sameness or routine to their ways. Instead, they randomly intruded into my peaceful surroundings with unpredictable loudness and motion creating chaos.

It took many years for me to get used to people. I did learn to tolerate them, but only when they could fit into my scheme of the world outside my skin (*Sky Glory Blue* and *Sky Glory Diamonds*). Initially, after noticing stranger-people—those not in my family—I began to figure out that the masses of people who made demands on me during the day outside my home were different people from the people at my house and in my neighborhood. Different people belonged to different places. Working these people into my schemata of sparkles and tails was how I was able to start to begin to incorporate other people as part of the world (*Sky Glory Day* and *Sky Glory Moon*).

Considerations When Working With Others

- New people in my space took getting used to. Typically when new people first come into the space of autistic children they start off by making demands on the children. Usually the child is brought to a therapy setting or to school or perhaps has in-home therapy. Something is supposed to happen during these paid appointments or in the educational setting.

However, if you try to abruptly introduce your agenda, you will probably be met with protest, especially if you are intrusive with your expectations. Give time for the child to accommodate you into the way they have made order and sense of the world around them. Practically, this means to give time without placing demands on the child for the child to get used to you and to accommodate your presence.

✓ What is your plan of action at your first encounter with a child with autism?

- The sparkles and tails I could see with my eyes were much more vibrant, interesting and predictable than people. I felt little need to interact with people. Therefore, if people wanted me to interact with them they had the best chance of success when they entered into my schemata of how I had the world sorted out. If they tried to catch sparkles with me I was much more likely to notice them.

  Entering into whatever is capturing a child's attention is a great way to forge a beginning relationship. Once you have established shared attention on something important to the child you can try to make that something even bigger and better so as to entice the child's engagement and enjoyment of you as a person.

  EXAMPLE: A boy named Sammy was intrigued with the sun shining in the window. It looked like he was trying to catch it. He would sometimes dance in the sunshine and other times stand right outside the sun's rays and cautiously stick a finger or a foot into the path of the sunshine. I danced with Sammy when he danced. I stood on the opposite side of the sunray and stuck my finger and my foot into the other side of the sunray in synchrony with Sammy. After three days Sammy began engaging with me. Soon I could make playful demands on him and a short time later he was able to allow me to engage him in learning activities that were clearly my agenda, not his. We came to enjoy each other.

    - ✓ How will you follow the lead of a child who is new to you when establishing engagement?

- Respect the experience of someone who experiences the world differently from the way you experience the world. We know when you consider our ways to be wrong and your goal is to fix us by forcing a behavior change. We also know when you respect us, consider our ways to be an interesting difference and you join with us offering new ideas and ways to solve our problems and make our life more comfortable. Please work with us, not on us.

    - ✓ How do you view your student? Do you consider him an interesting, lovable person or a project to be worked on?

    - ✓ What will you do to work with him rather than to work on him?

Intrusion

People came into my space

And I did notice them

    But paid no heed

    Lest I might lose

        My sparkle-catching

        Inward very being

One Person Tail

One Person Tail Intrusion

Two Person Tail Intrusion

Even
when
they
didn't
disrupt

my
sparkle tails
for
taking—

the
pain
they
brought

reflected
in

my
sun's
diminished
being.

Diminished Sun 1

Diminished Sun 2

Diminished Sun 3

An Aspect of My Autism

People sometimes thought I was stubborn and resistant when I did not seem to want to allow them into my space or to do what they wanted me to do. They did not understand the negative effect they had on me and on my surroundings. I had made sense out of the ever-present sparkles and tails I could see all around me. Other people disrupted that sense whenever I accommodated them by allowing them in my space or interacted with them.

I have illustrated this concept in a series of three paintings. *One Person Tail* depicts me standing in the world interacting with the world's tail. The tail is beautifully shaped and the pieces making up the tail are easy to see with clarity of shape, arc and color.

One Person Tail Intrusion illustrates the effect on the tail when I acknowledged the presence of one other person. I did not interact with this person, but merely acknowledged his presence by briefly glancing his way and then shared the space with him. While the general shape of the tail is still pleasant to look at you can see the clarity of the individual pieces has faded. Instead of one clear consistent color it has turned into three colors. Additionally, each piece is fuzzier in quality.

Two Person Tail Intrusion illustrates that when two other persons are acknowledged and allowed in my space, the top of the tail flattens as if there is not room enough for the tail to stretch out to form a beautiful shape. This happens whenever people need to take up space and attention. The colors of the tail shift to much less pleasant combinations of color that are bold and clash rather than harmonizing with one another. In addition, each piece making up the tail appears smudged and quite fuzzy.

The beauty of the world's tail is lost to me when more than one person intrudes on my space. Because I have learned the predictability, sameness and routine of the tails and used this as my anchor to make sense of the world, I could not allow the presence of too many people when I was a young child. When many people were forced on me the world became filled with confusion, chaos and change because I lost the tails that grounded me. When the tails were lost, so was my stability. It became quite scary.

My intent was not to be stubborn and resistant, even though I understand my behavior probably did look that way. My intent was to preserve the tails due to their accomplished function of predictability, sameness and routine for me. I needed this order in my world to enable me to participate and engage. Initially I could engage with one person at a time as that was not too disruptive. It took several years before I could engage with more than one person at a time and learn to become part of a small group.

Another way the presence and interaction with people affected me was the way in which it diminished my perception of the sun. If you compare the series of *Diminished Sun* paintings (*Diminished Sun 1*, *Diminished Sun 2*, and *Diminished Sun 3*) with the *Right Sun* and *Left Sun* paintings on pages 22 and 23 you can see the differences.

It was interesting to me that any number of people—whether it be one person, two people or more than two people—had the same diminished effect on my perception of the sun. This was different from the graduated affect one, two or more people had on my visual perception of the world's tails. Over time I understood that it worked better for me to track the sun sparkles rather than the world's tails when people arrived on the scene. It was less disruptive and allowed me to do more of what was asked of me in terms of participating in interactions with other people. Tracking sun sparkles rather than world tails allowed me to be a more flexible person.

Considerations When Working With Others

- Please know that the behavior of people with autism makes sense in the context of their experience of the world around them. Because neurotypical people do not share our context they are not often able to assign correct meaning and motivation to some of our behavior. They do their best by assigning meaning to our behavior based on what the behavior would mean were they themselves engaged in the behavior.

  Often they arrive at wrong conclusions. Sometimes they even assign negative character traits to us based on their wrong conclusions. In the example from my own childhood above you can see my intent was not to be stubborn and uncooperative by ignoring or not interacting with others, but instead was quite the opposite. I was trying to preserve the predictable order of the world in the only context available to me at the time—that of sun sparkles and world tails. I needed to do this IN ORDER TO ENGAGE WITH OTHERS.

  Therefore, try to refrain from assigning motive and meaning to the behavior of your student with autism based on what the behavior would mean were you engaged in it. Instead, assume that even though you may not understand it, the behavior makes sense to your student in the context of his experience of the world. This will allow you to more creatively solve problematic situations.

  - ✓ Will you please stop attributing willful bad behavior to autistics?

- It may be interesting to know that I am now in my late 50s and I have not shared the constructs of sun sparkles and world tails along with their importance in my early childhood until now. When I was a youngster I did not have the words to describe it.

  Even if I had the words and the ability to use those words to effectively communicate, I would not have understood to do so. How would I have known that others would be interested in this, or that this was a topic for conversation when I never heard anyone else talk about it?

  Know that even if you ask your student to explain why they are behaving the way they are behaving seldom will they be able to tell you. This isn't because they do not want to tell you, but is because they do not have a way to do so. Rather than being a matter of won't (as in "he won't tell me; he refuses to tell me") it is a matter of can't (as in "he does not have the language, the skills or the ability to tell me").

  - ✓ Will you please stop saying that autistics "refuse" or "won't" do something?

  - ✓ Will you come to understand that most of the time when people with autism don't do what you ask it is because they can't?

    Many times our neurology does not allow us to access the needed skill in the moment. I know this is very frustrating for you. It is very frustrating for us too.

Growing Up

Chapter Four: Accommodation

People Accommodation

Sometimes human beings

In my space cause havoc

Making World Tails

Too much, too scattered

In air space

And then

My heart is breaking.

Heartbreak Night Tail

Heartbreak Day Tail

An Aspect of My Autism

People generally are very pleased with themselves when they have made an accommodation for me. I know this because they proudly announce it! In turn, I have learned to say thank you when people announce their thoughtfulness at making an accommodation for me. I truly am thankful because it allows me a fuller participation in the events going on around me. It also makes me smile because I have been making accommodations for people my whole life and it has never occurred to me to announce it!

The fact is that autistics are required to make numerous accommodations every day they are among other people. This is because the world is not set up in a neurologically friendly way to autistics. We live in a very fast-paced world where speed in understanding and responding to people is expected. We also have much information constantly being delivered over numerous electronic devices. We expect everything to happen instantly!

For the most part this isn't a good match for people with autism because we generally have a "too much" experience of the world due to the way our sensory system takes in information from the world around us. Once that information "arrives" it is then, for many autistics, processed differently. A common result of our difference is referred to as a processing delay. This means it takes more time for us to process and respond. Not only is this a huge disadvantage in our fast-paced world of instant expectation, but one unspoken assumption is that I will accommodate for my differences and act "appropriately," i.e., act as a neurotypical acts.

It takes time and energy to accommodate another person regardless if you are the person with autism or the person without autism. Based on years of observation of numerous autistics, myself included, I can see autistics pay a much higher cost for the accommodations they must make as compared to the neurotypical person. Part of the reason is the sheer volume of accommodations an autistic is required to make each day compared to the NT. The irony is that autistics rarely are in any way acknowledged for the heavy burden of accommodations they must make just to survive in this world, while NTs are thought to be the people making the accommodations! Moreover, I am expected to make accommodations for you while you have the option to choose when, if, and how often you will make accommodations for me.

This differential is a result of assigning the measure of normal to the experience of the majority of the people. Even though I make considerably more accommodations for you than you make for me, because your experience of the world is considered the norm and my experience the deviation, it is the understanding of the majority that I need you to accommodate me and this is true. However, nobody notices all the accommodating I have done all my life!

Another ironic aspect about this whole accommodation situation is that when you accommodate me, even if you do not announce it, everybody considers you to be a really good person for making accommodations for an autistic. For you, making accommodations is not only optional, but when you do so you are considered a good person. For me, making accommodations is not optional. Because your ways are considered the norm I am expected to do whatever I need to do to act normal. For me, making accommodations for you is not optional. It is expected and, therefore, no credit given. In fact, the only time people notice me in regards to accommodations I make for them is when I neglect to make them!

When I cannot or do not make accommodations for you something is considered to be wrong with me. The double standard is that you are known as a good person for the accommodations you make for me while I can only be known as a bad person when I fail at making an accommodation for you. And just like you will not be thought of as a bad person when you fail to make an accommodation for me, I will never be thought of as a good person when I do make accommodations for you. At least this hasn't yet happened in my life even though I have made considerably more accommodations over the years for NTs than NTs will likely ever make for me!

I have learned that I am nearing my limit of my ability to make accommodations when my world tails start looking ragged (*Heartbreak Night Tail*) or too busy (*Heartbreak Day Tail*). It took me until my forties to recognize this. Now I know whenever my world tails start looking ragged or too busy it is time to wind up whatever I am doing and excuse myself for a time away from people. It means my ability to continue to make accommodations so I might fit into the world around me is almost over.

Considerations When Working With Others

- Accommodations are something provided by law to people with disabilities. It is easy to understand physical accommodations such as wheelchairs and curb cuts. It is much more difficult to understand accommodations when they involve sensory and processing differences such as those common to autistic people. Because an autism diagnosis is one of a spectrum diagnosis there are a variety of ways autistic people experience their particular autism. In fact, even though there may be similarities, no two autistics experience the world in exactly the same way. This makes it challenging because the necessary accommodations for one autistic will not be the same for the next autistic.

- ✓ Do you have a working definition of accommodations as provided by law to your students with disabilities?

- ✓ What accommodations are necessary for each of your students to receive an appropriate education as defined by law?

• Even though it may be hard work for you to support your student with autism by providing accommodations, please remember that your student is likely working at least as hard, if not harder than you, at accommodating you. I understand you think autism is hard. You are right. Autism can be very hard.

- ✓ What accommodations do your students routinely make for you?

• Please respect the downtime or break time you give us as an accommodation. Many people do not understand how much work it can be for autistics to accommodate the talking of neurotypicals. When you talk to us during our downtime it negates the accommodation you are attempting to make for us.

- ✓ How can you give your student downtime or a sensory break that is truly a time away from the demands of accommodating a NT world?

Look Me In the Eye

"Look me in the eye," they say.

    Too much, too bright, too big, too bold

Look Me In the Eye

The piercing burning pokes from them

    STRIKE ME   Lightning bolts

      Straight-shot from their eyes

        Right on into mine.

            SIZZLE, POP

        They slice on through

                My very being—

                BUZZING BONES

                      The painful hurt

              Each time I try obeying.

Buzzing Bones

Eye Fish

The way too much of it

    Searing through

    My soul like death

    Erasing world beauty.

Yet, with smiling lips   I float right through my skin

    And eyes   Avoiding

    Obedient—   Too much, too bright

    Looking where they're told—   Too big, too bold.

SIZZLE POP

Employing ceiling hovering

    Watching down below—

        That other girl

        With smiling lips

        And correctly gazing eyes—

            While I myself get busy

            From my ceiling perch

            Up high—

Eye Trees

Eye Land

SIZZLE, POP—

And then

Eye shapes

I elsewhere find!

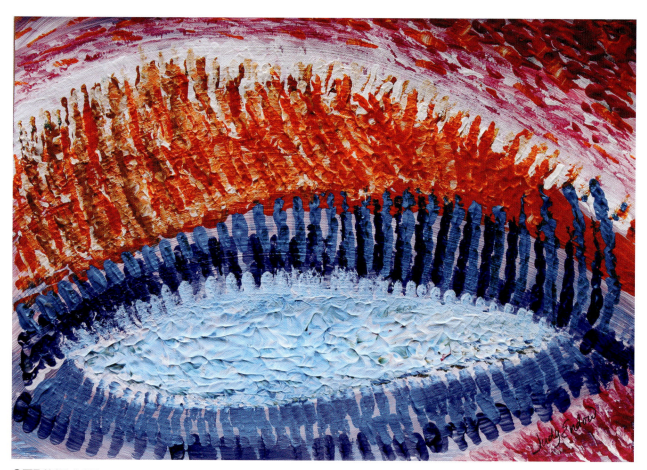

STRIKE ME

    It came to pass

        When "Look me in the eye,"

    They said

        I did so quite correctly.

        It cost us both—

            We pay the price.

            STRIKE ME!

                With my dime they buy their candy.

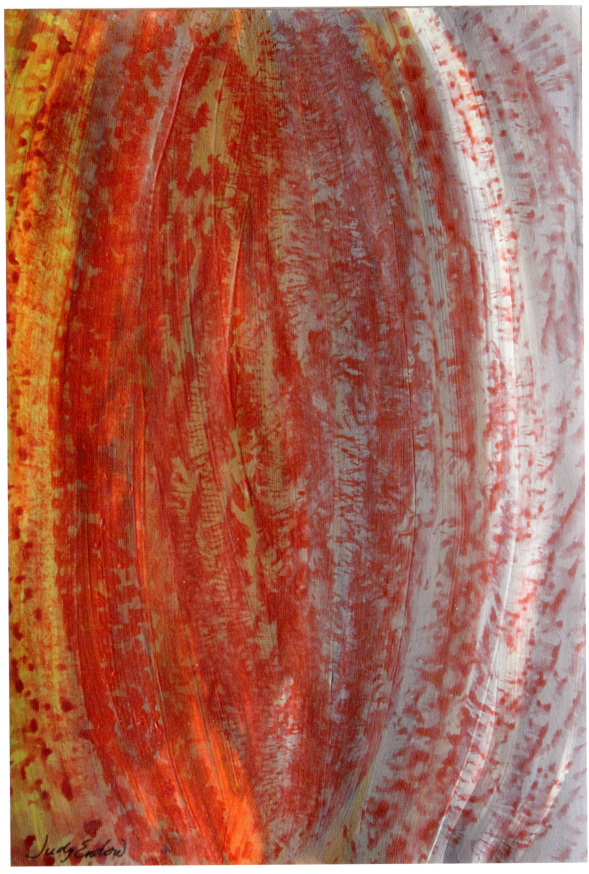

Eye Tulip

After that, when "Look me in the eye,"

    They said

    I'd float

        Straight way to

        The ceiling.

            I'd watch some eyes—

                Look right at them—

                My newfound

                    Eye-shaped

                    Ceiling bootie!

Goldenrod 2

Goldenrod 3

Goldenrod 4

An Aspect of My Autism

Eye contact can be hard for some autistics for a variety of reasons. When I was a young child I received too much bright, bold, painful sensory information when directly looking into someone's eyes for a sustained period of time (*Look Me In the Eye, Buzzing Bones, SIZZLE POP,* and *STRIKE ME*). I learned to cope by disengaging from the experience. I would hover up by the ceiling and watch the girl below who was me. When the girl looked into the eyes of people I would use the too much information she got to fashion alternatives to those eyes that would cut down on the overwhelming sensory information (*Eye Fish, Eye Trees, Eye Land,* and *Eye Tulip*).

Donna Williams has described the experience of dissociation (Williams; website accessed 2013): Dissociation is the ability to cut off from what is happening around you or to you. In its simplest form it is daydreaming. It is a skill all children have and which children with autism tend to overdevelop in managing a world they find overwhelming for a whole range of reasons. The more dissociative experiences I had, the more refined my creations from eye information became. In the *Goldenrod* series one might not even realize the information originally came from eye contact. However, once pointed out most people notice the eye shape in the background (*Goldenrod 2, Goldenrod 3,* and *Goldenrod 4*).

Today I am able to use eye contact in a pretty typical manner most of the time. The sensory information I pick up from engaging in eye contact is not often painful. I have noticed that my sensory needs have changed over time. However, even today when I am under stress I do not have typical eye contact. Avoiding eye contact is one of the things I find myself automatically doing to minimize the quantity of incoming sensory information.

Considerations When Working With Others

- Some children with autism have difficulty engaging in typical eye contact and some children with autism don't. This is not a willful, planned behavior. Think about the numerous times you employ eye contact. Do you willfully think each time prior to looking at another person about the fact that you are planning to look at that person? Of course not! It is like that for people with autism who avoid eye contact. We do not ahead of time willfully plan to avoid looking at someone. We simply don't do it in the same manner that you simply do it. It is the way our brains do business.

Imagine how you might feel if you were asked to stop looking at people—to cease all eye contact. Now imagine how much more difficult that would be if each time you did manage not to engage in eye contact you felt physical pain and the only way to relieve that pain was to look at the person even though you knew it would make others unhappy. This is often what we put children through when we insist they go against the way their brain does business by forcing them to use typical eye contact.

- ✓ Does your child have atypical eye contact?

- ✓ Is it important to you to insist your child employ typical eye contact even if you knew it might cause him physical pain?

- ✓ Are you willing to put off teaching your child the importance of eye contact, knowing it may be easier and less painful for him to engage in eye contact as he grows older, as his sensory system will likely experience some maturation over time?

• Sometimes engaging in eye contact is important, especially as children grow up into teens and adults. When people do not look someone in the eye they can be thought of as shifty, sneaky or disinterested. Autistics can be taught alternatives to use when looking someone in the eye is painful for them. One alternative is to glance at the eyebrows rather than the eyes of your conversation partner. It is good to practice this during a conversation as faulty timing can send an entirely different social message than the one you are intending to send. Watching video clips of people engaging in eye contact during conversation is often helpful.

If eye contact remains so uncomfortable as to avoid altogether you may want to come up with a script to use for situations where you would want to explain why you are avoiding eye contact so people will not attribute something to you that is not true socially.

- ✓ At what point do you think it important to teach your child eye contact alternatives?

- ✓ Will you help your child develop a short script he might use to explain his lack of eye contact?

- ✓ How will you teach your child when to employ alternative eye contact methods and/or when to use his explanatory script?

Beauty-Eyes Beholding

Over time when "Look me in the eye"

    They said,

    While hovering

    Near the ceiling,

Snow Melting

I'd hear their colors

See their sounds and

Track their moves around me—

Spring Hill

Soon I could put

    Their soul-good in

        My PICTURE TREE

            And in

                GROUNDSCAPE

                    And in AIR.

AIRSCAPE

GROUNDSCAPE

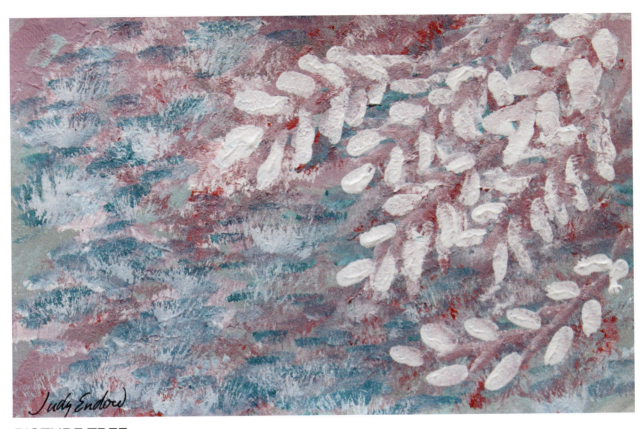
PICTURE TREE

And thus I came to know

    The goodness in

    That floor parade

    Of stilted human beings.

Goodness Bay

Goodness Hills

Goodness Tree

An Aspect of My Autism

Neurotypical people report they learn much information by looking into the eyes of others. The saying "eyes are the window to the soul" is never debated, but instead assumed to be a universal truth. I do not get this sort of information about other people by looking into their eyes. In fact, when I do look into their eyes I am least able to get any kind of information. The task of looking at their eyes takes so much of my attention and personal resources that I am unable to also decipher and attribute any sort of social meaning embedded in the gaze of a conversation partner. The harder I try and the longer I look the worse this becomes!

Just because I do not get information about others through looking at their eyes, it doesn't mean that I do not pick up this sort of nonverbal social information about them. I get this information through the colors that I perceive emanating from people (*AIRSCAPE, GROUNDSCAPE,* and *PICTURE TREE*). These colors change as circumstances change so I am not able to answer when people, after learning of my color perception, approach and ask with great expectation, "What color am I?" Specifically, the colors I perceive have sound and movement to them that are interactive with the colors. And it is in this interaction that I pick up much meaning about other people as they relate to me. Instead of looking in their eyes I notice the sound and movement of their colors as they interact with me (*Goodness Bay, Goodness Hills,* and *Goodness Tree*).

When people learn of my different way of perceiving them they are often intrigued. Because my way is novel to them they tend to attribute more to it than is warranted or even practical. They somehow think that my way is magical or superior. It is not. Most of the time I pick up enough good information to base decisions on, just like you do when you use eye contact. And just like with attributing character, intent and meaning based on eye contact, drawing these conclusions based on the ways of the colors sometimes leads to incorrect guesses or assumptions. My ways are not magical, just different!

It is interesting to me that people will ask my opinion on a matter and then somehow blame me on the occasions when my opinion turns out to be incorrect. They say things like, "So much for your colors!" or "Those colors give you no special insight!" I totally agree! I have never attributed to myself any sort of special insight due to gaining my information from the sound and movement of people's colors, but others tend to make special attribution to this because it is different from the standard eye contact way of picking up this sort of information. I really don't understand why I am to be somehow blamed for faulty conclusions drawn from my perception of colors as if it were a character flaw any more than you would act like people had some sort of willful character flaw when they guess wrong based on information they pick up through eye contact. I only know it happens and other people somehow blame me when this happens as if I have claimed a special power I do not possess, when in fact I have never thought, much less claimed, any special power or understanding.

Considerations When Working With Others

- Not everyone picks up information about other people in the same way. One way most people learn about others is through the use of eye contact. When people do not use eye contact, or use eye contact but are not able to pick up much information through its use, they likely have another way to learn about people.

    I learn about others through my perception of the sound and movement of colors emanating from them. Some autistics pick up information by using their senses in other unique ways. This is entirely reasonable when you consider that our sensory system generally is able to pick up greater quantity and greater detail than the sensory system of a neurotypical person. It only makes sense that our brains would use this to our benefit.

    If your child does not get information about others through the use of eye contact, and if you can answer "yes" to one or more of the following questions, I would venture to guess your child has another way, other than through the use of eye contact, to pick up information about other people:

    - ✓ Does your child sometimes notice other people?
    - ✓ Does you child sometimes show a preference for specific people?
    - ✓ Does your child connect particular people to certain activities?
    - ✓ Does your child have specific expectations tied to specific people?
    - ✓ Does your child tolerate the presence of some people, but react negatively to the presence of other people?

- ✓ Does your child interact willingly with some people, but ignore other people?

- If you answered "yes" to any of the above questions, know that even though your child could not in a million years explain to you how he picks up information about other people, he does in fact pick up information about other people! This is reflected in a child's preference for certain people, his ability to connect specific activities and/or expectations to particular people or his willingness to tolerate the presence of or interact with some people, but not others.

Forcing a child to do something that is helpful to you, such as using eye contact, will not necessarily do for a child with autism what it does for you! Our different neurology often prevents our brain from using the same source or kind of information your brain uses to extract similar benefits. Instead, we do business differently. This isn't right or wrong. It is different. Even so, it is just as valid for us as your method is for you!

Autistics are often comfortable with sharing a space without talking to one another and are often happy to each engage in solo activities in a shared space. When NTs in charge see this they often try to get us to interact with one another in the ways that are pleasurable for them to engage with friends, rather than to honor our way of engaging in relationships that we find meaningful. They assume the only way to make friends and be friends is by using the behavior they use to carry on in friendships. If we do not act in the ways they act they typically do not allow us access to our friends only because they do not understand or see that a meaningful friendship has developed.

- ✓ Even though your child may gather information about people in a different way than you gather information, will you respect decisions and preferences he makes based on the information he gathers whether or not you can understand it?

- ✓ Will you be on the lookout for relationships between your child and others even though they may be hard to recognize because they may look different from typical relationships?

- ✓ Will you support authentic relationship development between your child and other children even though it may look different from typical relationships?

EXAMPLE: Two autistics in the adult program had developed a friendship with one another. When Mark petted the therapy dog, Ryan watched from the other side of the room. When Ryan played CDs on his boombox he noticed Mark sometimes covered his ears and other times rocked to the beat of the music.

Most days Mark experienced difficulty feeding himself at lunchtime (a task he could physically do, but was exhausting for him). Ryan would choose a music CD he knew Mark liked and turn his boom box towards Mark.

Because there were several occupied lunch tables in-between Mark and Ryan, nobody realized that Ryan was helping Mark. In fact, nobody knew Ryan and Mark had become friends. They could not tell because the friendship behavior between Ryan and Mark looked different from that of NT friends.

After Ryan was moved to another group he lost interest in participating in activities and did not seem to enjoy things that he usually enjoyed like playing CDs on his boombox. He appeared depressed.

In the meantime Mark had altogether stopped attempting to feed himself, regressing so much that staff needed to feed him at lunchtime if he were to eat. One day the adult program had to change the lunchtimes of the various groups to accommodate one of the group's outing for the day. It put Mark and Ryan in the cafeteria at the same time.

Once in the lunchroom, Ryan, who had since quit carrying around his boombox and rarely played CDs on it anymore, asked for and used his boombox and CDs. Mark fed himself that day even though he had not even been asked to do so. An astute staff person noticed Ryan turning his boombox away from himself and also heard the staff across the room talking about how wonderful it was that Mark was feeding himself. Acting on a hunch, this staff person asked if Ryan's group could continue eating at the same time as Mark's group.

It was discovered that Mark and Ryan not only had been friends for many months, but when Ryan had been moved to another group both young men suffered the results of losing all access to this meaningful friendship. Arrangements were made for Ryan and Mark to eat lunch at the same time and to spend part of each day in the same room. Even though nobody could tell by looking, Mark and Ryan were the best of friends!

People Inclusion

But other times

A human being

    Can come into

    My spaces

        Of sunshine-sparkle

        World Tails

            That I see

            All around me—

                Not disrupting—

                They join me—

                My different ways embracing!

Dawn Inclusion Making

Twilight Inclusion Making

Dusk Inclusion Making

People Break

People in my space

    I came to tolerate

And then

        Much practice later

        Could reciprocate

Hard work, hard work, hard work

All the whole day long

        And yet I so sometimes enjoy

        These people in my space

            Connecting with their moving colors

            I do so much like doing!

            And even so it is

            Hard work, hard work, hard work

            For me

            So people breaks

            Need taking.

Girl on Dock

An Aspect of My Autism

Over time not only did I come to tolerate people better, but came to enjoy them! Today I enjoy traveling to new places and meeting new people as I fulfill my commitments for speaking engagements. I never thought I would actually be able to do the traveling or the meeting lots of new people aspects of public speaking, so it is amazing to me that I can enjoy it!

I had a learning curve related to public speaking. I had many trips where I could learn one aspect of travel at a time, repeat the experience and then go on to learn and repeat another aspect. Eventually, I learned enough that I no longer needed to be in learning mode each trip. Critical mass had developed! (For discussion on critical mass, see page 54.) This reduced my anxiety and allowed me to notice people. I discovered that even strangers could be interesting people to have for dinner companions!

Having an autism spectrum diagnosis means that there are difficulties with communication and with social understanding. This means social occasions are often difficult. It does not mean we are not social beings! A common scenario I see in schools involves an autistic student having a meltdown during a classroom holiday party followed by this student being provided an alternative activity during subsequent classroom parties. This is done because adults recognize how difficult the demands of a classroom party can be on a student with autism.

I would like to point out that just because something is difficult does not necessarily mean that we do not want to participate! One time two autistic friends and I were at a party in another friend's home. There were lots of people and much commotion. The hostess showed my friends and me a bedroom she invited us to use should we want to have a quiet break at any time during the party. This meant the world to us because we were given the means to accommodate our need for a few minutes of quiet should the party atmosphere become too overwhelming. Having this option allowed us freedom to participate fully in the party because the truth is that we like parties too! And even though parties are hard for us, with optimal supports available we can enjoy them too!

Sometimes I am able to participate in only a portion of a party or event rather than being in attendance the entire time. Sometimes I choose to do a planned late arrival and other times I leave early. There are many variables to social events and most of them are beyond anybody's control. It takes some planning and effort on my part, but I have found ways that work for me to include others in my space and in my life (*Dawn Inclusion Making, Twilight Inclusion Making,* and *Dusk Inclusion Making*). Today I have many friends.

One thing important for me in my ability to maintain friendships is to have considerable time alone (*Girl on Dock*). I live alone and have a very quiet home life. I rarely run the TV for more than 30-60 minutes at a time and I do not listen to music in my home. I do go to hear the symphony, enjoy musicals and ballets and find them more to my suiting than having constant music in my home or car, or to see a movie in a theater. When my children were all at home I did not have the luxury of a quiet house and did not enjoy the degree of regulation I am able to enjoy today. A lesser degree of regulation meant a lesser degree of participation and, consequently, many years of very few friends.

Considerations When Working With Others

- When events such as classroom parties are difficult for students it often seems kind to excuse them from parties. But what if they like parties and just do not have the skills and accommodations to negotiate a party NT style? Rather than an all or none attendance at a party, perhaps something in-between might work out better for an autistic participant.

    Many times special games are played at children's parties such as Pin the Tail on the Donkey that are never played at other times. A child with autism may need to learn how to play this game ahead of time in order to participate in playing at the party.

    - ✓ Does your child need to become familiar with aspects of a party before actually going to a party?
    - ✓ Might your child enjoy a party if he had the skills needed at a party?
    - ✓ Will you ensure your child has a quiet place to retreat to during a party when he needs it?

- I think we make a big mistake by counting a party or event a success only when the autistic participates in the same way an NT participates.

    EXAMPLE: I worked with Darien, a young man who kept asking me to tell his staff to take him to the park. His staff reported he hated the park. Upon further investigation I discovered Darien enjoyed the park differently than the staff expected he would enjoy the park. To assist staff in understanding this concept and to ensure they would in fact bring Darien to the park, I made a data collection sheet where staff would record after each park outing HOW Darien enjoyed the park. Options included enjoying the park by sitting in the car with the windows down, sitting on the bench at the park entrance, taking pictures of the park and walking in the park. This helped staff to count going to the park as enjoyable and successful for Darien even though it might not always look that way to an NT. The important thing here was Darien enjoyed a half-hour at the park even on the days he wasn't able to leave the car and staff needed to count this enjoyment as success rather than labeling it as failure and using it to decide Darien did not like going to the park!

- ✓ Do you use an NT yardstick to measure your autistic student's enjoyment of an activity?
- ✓ How will you determine whether or not your autistic student enjoys an activity or event when he behaves in a way different from an NT who enjoys it behaves?

LIVING

Living

Chapter Five: Thinking

Thinking Colors

My thinking is all in pictures
And in colors too.
    Always a front row seat I have
    To watch
        My moving color shows!

Each color, with variety
Unending in its hues
    Comprised of brightness variegated
    Is a master of its soul
        Delivering right to me
        Its living sound
            And moving color
            Combinations!

To think for me
Is but to watch
    These moving sounds
    And hear
        The colors of
        Thought picture
            Combinations.

I look up at that screen
Inside my mind
    Nurturing picture's
    Beauty sounds and looks
        Until my thought's completed.

Then interpret into words
I must
    If needed
    To communicate
        With various other people.

By painting
I can show
    My thoughts
    Circumventing burdens of
        Constant word translations.

Arctic Waves

Lavender-Tan Wave

Orange Wave

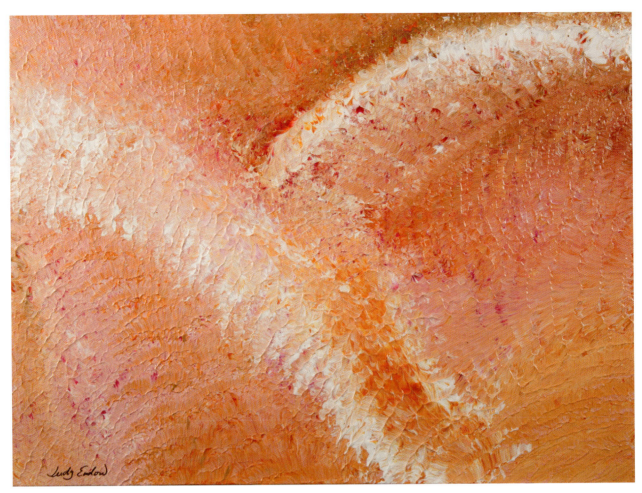
Orange-Pink White Wave

Bright Surf

Hawaii Surf

An Aspect of My Autism

I think differently than NT people think. Many people with autism have a visual way of thinking. It is not an inferior way of thinking. It is just different. Even so, because autistics are measured according to our deviation from the typical standard of normal our different ways are often assumed to be inferior or less than.

This is another example of why it is not helpful to think of autistic people in terms of their diagnosis. Because a diagnosis is based on deviation from accepted normal, an autism diagnosis shows a picture of what autistics ARE NOT and highlights what we CANNOT DO as compared to the majority normal. A diagnosis says nothing at all about the human beings we ARE or what we CAN DO.

Our abilities and skills often remain unnoticed and untapped. The majority of the people in the world do not posses our autistic skills and abilities. Because of this they do not notice them and really do not have a good way to understand them. This makes it nearly impossible for NTs to support autistic skill development in us. For example, if my way of thinking in the movement and sound of color had been understood by those around me and then supported over my growing up years, I likely would have been able to produce paintings well before my 50s (*Arctic Waves* and *Lavender-Tan Wave*).

Please remember the measure of autism is one of "less than" as a diagnostic necessity, but we are not "less than" human beings. We have a diagnosis—not a flawed humanity. We have a different operating system. We have a different way of experiencing the world (*Orange Wave* and *Orange-Pink Wave*). We have a different way of thinking (*Bright Surf* and *Hawaii Surf*). This means we may struggle with many of your ways and have to overcome many obstacles to fit into the way the world runs, but we are not less than—
just different.

Considerations When Working With Others

- When interacting with an autistic, think of that person rather than what you happen to know about autism. What you know about autism may or may not apply to the person with whom you are interacting. And even if it does apply, it will not do much for you in terms of getting to know that person.

    - ✓ Do you use words to describe your student according to the purpose of your conversation?

> EXAMPLE: When planning an educational program a student's deficits are typically discussed because it is relevant to a learning plan that needs to be figured out. When planning a classroom party a student's skills and abilities, what activities he enjoys and who he is friends with are likely more important than his deficits.

- Get to know us for who we are and for what we can do rather than for the diagnostic criteria attached to our label. This may be hard because the majority of social conversation and news media reporting is laden with definitions of autism, which of necessity are deficit-based. Unfortunately, this is what people have come to know about autism. It has become our "public image" so to speak.

    - ✓ Do you know your student's favorite activities, foods to eat or toys to play with?

    - ✓ Do you understand what makes your student happy, sad, excited, etc?

    - ✓ Do you know what your student is able to do outside of school?

Inflexible Thinking

Autism lives
    in the   Place of Here.

Transition continually
demands of Autism, "Go There."

    every day
Autism has

      Such a   hard time

    figuring things   out

    because
      you see

    it is

      very difficult

    to get

    to Planet Go There
      in her Car of Wait…

To facilitate
    Autism getting
      her Car of Wait

    over the border
      into the place

      of the space of
        Planet Go There

    give her
      lots of permission
      to STOP
        when she's Stuck

                    and   to WAIT
                            'til she's   safe

which is contrary
    to the ways
    of the world

            but   if done
        consistently

                over and   over

will help
    Autism get   to
    Planet Go There

            and ultimately
            one day

                    to take up   residence

                to live
                in her   place

                        in your world.

Excerpted from *Making Lemonade: Hints for Autism's Helpers*, pp. 78-92 (Endow 2006).

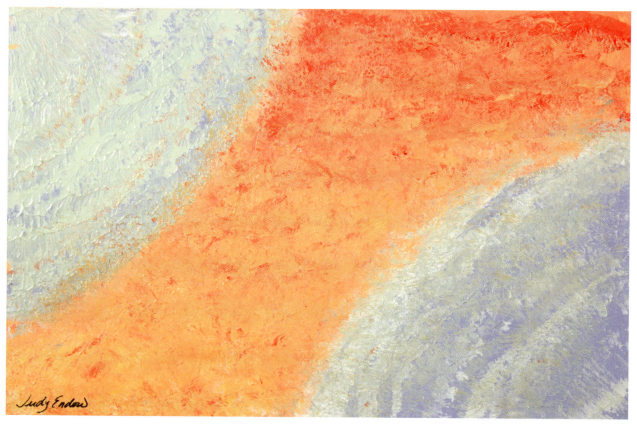
Planetary Sky Upper Left

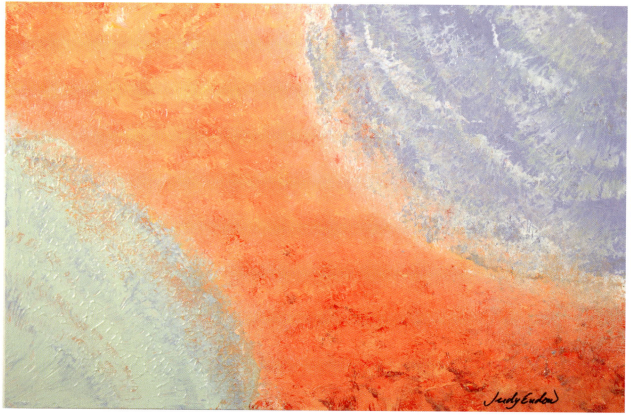
Planetary Sky Lower Left

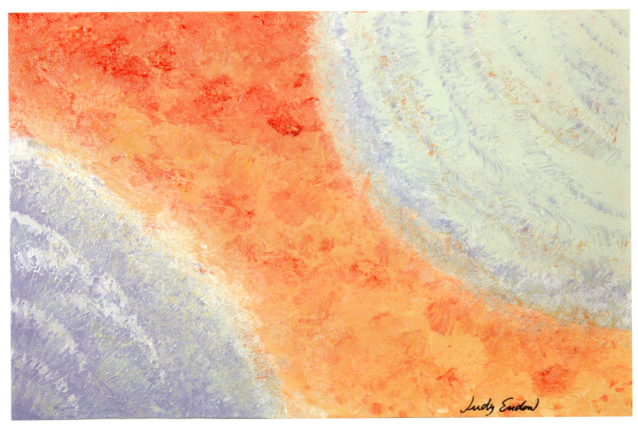
Planetary Sky Upper Right

Planetary Sky Lower Right

An Aspect of My Autism

Sometimes people say I have inflexible thinking. If they are less kind they describe me as stubborn, obstinate, or demanding my own way.

Planetary Sky illustrates one way I have worked with my neurology to acquire a more flexible way of thinking over the years. The four separate pieces, arranged as you see them, represent an original thought (*Planetary Sky Upper Left, Planetary Sky Lower Left, Planetary Sky Upper Right,* and *Planetary Sky Lower Right*).

The four pieces can be arranged in a multitude of ways to show how picture thoughts can be adjusted. Sometimes part of a thought may need to be "turned over"—literally turning that painting over so the backside shows. The literal "turning over" is what I need to do in order to make room in my thoughts to consider an alternative.

Learning how to move parts of my thoughts and how to "turn over" other parts has paved the way for me to be thought of by others as a more flexible person, no longer so stubborn, obstinate or demanding.

Considerations When Working With Others

- People with autism are often described as "inflexible," whether it is in reference to the way they think or in reference to how they act. This difference is often based in their operating system—the way their brain does business. Because it is different from the NT way of managing in the world, we use "inflexible" to describe this as different from the NT norm of a more "flexible" way of thinking and behaving. The words we use have power (Endow 2009b) to shape how we think and feel about situations and people. They also have much power in determining how we go about problem solving or remaining stuck in difficult situations.

    - ✓ Does using the term "inflexible" in reference to how your child thinks or behaves help you to solve the dilemma of your child being stuck?

    - ✓ Does using the term "inflexible" in reference to how your child thinks or behaves propel you into a feeling of hopelessness in terms of you ever being able to positively impact this difficult situation?

    - ✓ If the language you currently use is not helpful, what might you substitute so as to be more helpful?

- It is much easier to work with a person's way of thinking than to simply define it as "wrong." It took me until in my 40s to accept the fact that my inflexibility was an NT construct that was not so helpful to me in terms of being able to navigate the world around me. When I began to honor my visual way of thinking, I was able to work with it in terms of achieving a way to incorporate a different idea or a change of plans.

  Visual thinkers usually need a visual way to change their thinking in order to adjust for new plans or to incorporate other people's ideas into their own thinking. There are numerous ways autistics do this with some commonalities, and with some novel and individually unique ways having been reported.

  One common example I've run into is that visual thinkers often have a visual way to start and stop thinking about things. This might include visualizing, filing an idea into a filing drawer cabinet or putting it into a document folder on their computer. Some find the idea of parking their thoughts in a parking lot or a garage helpful. This is important to understand because a visual thinker will often be unable to simply stop thinking about something without actually visually putting the thought (which is usually in pictures) in a physical location where it can stay until needing to be retrieved at a later time. Much thinking labeled "OCD" in autistics can be managed this way.

  - ✓ Has your child found helpful visual ways to support a change in plans or to incorporate other people's ideas?

  - ✓ If your child is a visual thinker, does he have a visual way to stop thinking about something—a visual place to "file" or "park" a thought so he won't lose it and can later retrieve it?

- Showing a change in the line up of daily activities can be accomplished efficiently by showing it on a student's visual schedule because the showing supports the student's visual way of thinking. Using an interactive visual schedule is a good place to begin in terms of getting to better understand and support your student's visual thinking (Endow 2011).

  In addition, it is important to understand how your particular student thinks so you might show him how to work with incorporating new ideas and change in a way that makes sense to him. Once he knows how to do this and has had some practice, he will appear to be much more flexible!

- ✓ If your child were to change his thinking about something, how would that look to him?

- ✓ Once you understand how your child's thinking looks and works for him, what are some ways you might support him to visually move around his thoughts? (The neurological movement that occurs during thinking is what allows for flexibility.)

- ✓ Might you construct a visual that would show your child how to get his thoughts to move and take new shapes, colors and/or appearances? (This is an example of visual thinking language.)

Thought Waves

The sound

And movement

Of colors

IS

The "stuff" of my thinking

Moving parts

And color sounds

Is what I watch

When contemplating

What you are saying

Or in private

Is a generation of complex idea thinking

A moving, sounding, mesmerizing,

extrapolating process

Is my thought wave

Time taking

Color thinking

White Thought Wave on Earth-Fire

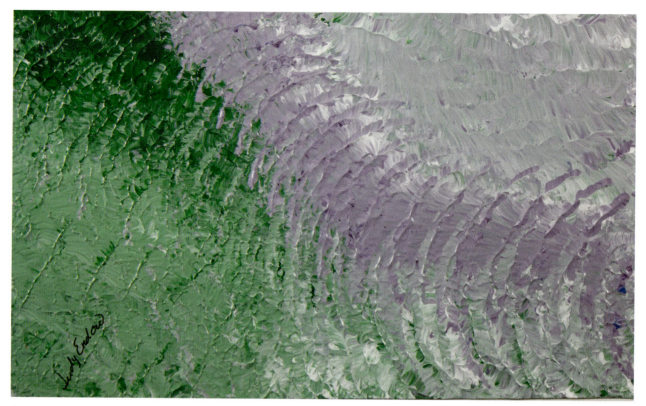

Lavender Thought Wave on Green

White-Pink Thought Wave on Orange

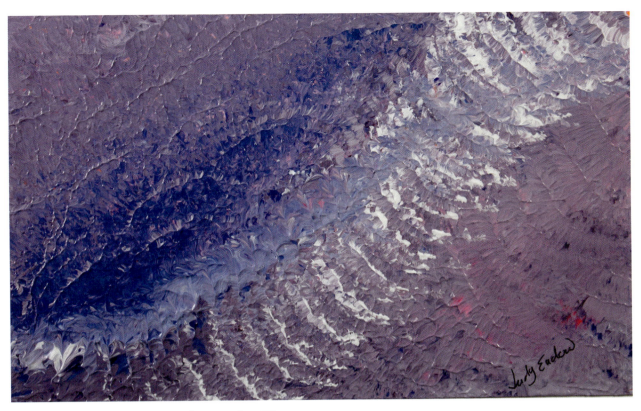

White Thought Wave on Lavender Blues

White Thought Wave on Green

An Aspect of My Autism

When people talk to me my brain responds by automatically creating and matching an internal thought wave to the words I hear (*Lavender Thought Wave on Green* and *White-Pink thought Wave on Orange*). Even though spoken words are the medium most often used by people to communicate with me, I am wired to connect to these words through the sound and movement of colors. And, my neurology automatically goes for the match while I watch. Once the thought wave is stable enough I can translate it into words (*White Thought Wave on Lavender Blues* and *White Thought Wave on Green*).

This is the way I think (*White Thought Wave on Earth-Fire*). It moves quite fast, but even so, tends to be slower than the speed of conversation. Because speed is so valued by society, we tend to give people no more than a few seconds to respond to our spoken words.

When my way of processing requires a few extra moments, instead of understanding my way of thinking might have some valuable aspects to it, people only see that my verbal response is different in speed from the accepted standard of normal. My difference takes on the negative, deviation-from-the-norm language because people are always measured by the standard of majority that we all adopt as normal. Thus, measured with an NT yardstick, people describe me as having processing delays. Based on these delays they often go on to decide I am less intelligent.

Considerations When Working With Others

- Many times, even though processing delays are attributed to autistics, people working with them do not change their behavior to accommodate for processing delays. Instead they often assume the autistic is less intelligent because he does not have an immediate response.

    - ✓ If you increase response time for academic work will your autistic student show an increase in accurate responding?

    - ✓ If you allow for longer pauses in conversation will your student respond more often?

    - ✓ How might you use visual support of your spoken directions to see if your student's number and/or accuracy of response to verbal directives increase?

- If your student has normal or above normal intelligence and appears less intelligent due to a processing delay, it is important that your student come to understand that he is indeed intelligent. It is also important he know what supports need to be in place for him to access his responses efficiently and how to effectively explain his processing differences and supports to others. Without this your student will be hampered in being able to maintain access to and to negotiate relationships with other human beings.

- ✓ Is your student's self-concept based on erroneous assumed-by-others "facts" about him?

- ✓ Is your student's self-concept based on his own made-up negative stories he uses in his head to explain his differences to himself?

- ✓ What supports are helpful to your student in terms of mitigating effects of processing delays? (Common supports and accommodations include increased time and visual directions in conjunction with verbal directions.)

- ✓ Would it be helpful for your student to have a script to explain his processing delays to himself (to replace negative self-talk) and/or to others?

    If the script is to be used with others, please include in the script what you want others to do in response to the information about the processing delay, such as to give a few moments longer pause during conversation, etc.

- ✓ If your student has a script to explain his processing delay, will you provide time to practice implementation of using this script?

Living

Chapter Six: Processing

Blue-Green Leaves

Is this one real?
Or maybe
    it's this one?

    Or that one
    Or that one
    Or that one?

        I really do not know.

    But each time I
    I take a look outside
    When sunshine's bright all 'round

        To see the leaves upon the trees

        They look this way
        That way

        And then another
        Another
        And still another

        'til

            I am not sure
            I do not know

            Just how
            Real leaves
            On trees
            Outside
            My window
            look.

5th Blue-Green Leaves

1st Blue-Green Leaves

3rd Blue-Green Leaves

2nd Blue-Green Leaves

4th Blue-Green Leaves

An Aspect of My Autism

This series of five paintings (*1st Blue-Green Leaves, 2nd Blue-Green Leaves, 3rd Blue-Green Leaves, 4th Blue-Green Leaves,* and *5th Blue-Green Leaves*) illustrates how looking at the same view five times can produce five different results. Whenever there is artificial lighting there is a chance my eyes will play this trick on me! It sometimes happens in natural lighting too, but less often than in artificial lighting.

The tricky part is that this experience may or may not happen on a given day. It is unpredictable. When it does happen my movement, of necessity, becomes very focused and deliberate as my surroundings are perceived to be in flux with stable items in transit and moving components, such as people walking, being fractured visually—thus I see people poofing away like a white ball dandelion being poofed into the wind while furniture, walls, buildings and sidewalks appear to move. When I was younger I did not know that furniture and buildings did not move on their own! I did not know which of my experiences were real and which ones were illusions. To me, they were all real. I had no way of knowing.

Considerations When Working With Others

- Many with autism have movement difficulties. There are numerous ways movement difficulties can play out in any given person. There can be troubles in the areas of starting, stopping, executing, continuing, combining or switching. The "troubles" in executing movement have to do with factors of speed, intensity, rhythm, timing, direction and duration. All these variables can combine in numerous ways impacting postures, actions, speech, thoughts, perceptions, emotions and memories (Leary and Donnellan 2012). It is no wonder so many autistics act in ways NTs do not, or display behaviors often labeled as "unusual."

    - ✓ Might the "unusual" movements displayed by your child be due to a movement difference?

    - ✓ What supports might you put in place to accommodate a movement difference?

    - ✓ How might implementation of a movement-related support or intervention be different from trying to change the unwanted behavior of an autistic?

✓ Do you notice a shift in your own attitude when replacing the idea of bad behavior with the idea of movement disorder?

EXAMPLE: Lamar would line up with his third grade class and go to music, gym, out to recess and pretty much anywhere the students went except to the lunchroom. Lamar would start out walking in his place in line, but as soon as he turned the corner he would stop walking toward the lunchroom.

In fact, the only way anyone could get him to walk was to allow him to turn around and walk away from the lunchroom. Lamar had eaten in this same lunchroom during first and second grade and nothing about the lunchroom had changed. People guessed all sorts of reasons for Lamar's behavior and had tried numerous interventions that all failed to get Lamar into the lunchroom.

I went along with the line of children going to the lunchroom. I noticed when the problematic corner was turned there was a change in lighting. All the school's hallway lighting was overhead fluorescent lights except in the short hallway outside the lunchroom when approached from the west side of the building.

My guess was that the difference from overhead fluorescent lighting to the globe lighting along the walls was what was causing Lamar to stop walking. We got these lights turned off to test it out, but it did not make a difference!

Next, I noticed the pattern on the floor changed. It was a subtle change, but there was a visually noticeable crack between the two floors where a newer part of the building had been added on. The actual crack had been filled in so in reality there was no crack—only the appearance of a crack. The floor pattern was the same but slightly lighter in the newer section of the building on the other side of the crack.

The gym was close, so one of the instructors borrowed a tumbling mat from the gym to place over the crack thinking that the mat would make a visual bridge from one floor pattern over the crack to the next floor pattern.

We were all delighted when Lamar made it to the lunchroom! It did make us giggle because after three adults modeled walking on the mat over to the lunchroom, when it was Lamar's turn he did somersaults across the mat! Even though the mat was not in the gym, tumbling in the gym was the context for the mat that Lamar was familiar with!

Eventually, the school got a heavy indoor/outdoor rug with rubber backing to put on the floor that stayed there and all the students walked on it. This is but one example of a movement-related challenge.

- I have come across several students with autism at various locations across my state that favor using portable laptops over desktop computers. As the numbers increased I began to realize this might be more than a preference.

Around this same time I bought my first laptop. I was amazed at how much longer I could work on the laptop as compared to a desktop computer! I was not bothered by what looked like light balls randomly flickering across the screen after fifteen minutes, and my eyes did not water.

Because I experienced such a difference, I looked into the matter. I discovered that laptops use a different behind-the-screen technology than desktop computers and for my autism it was a huge positive difference! I realized that laptop use was more of a need than a preference by some of my students!

✓ When your student with autism shows a preference for certain materials do you consider that what looks like a preference might actually be a need?

✓ Do you know that accommodations are needs and not preferences?

✓ Do you become concerned that it might not be fair to other students if Haley always gets to use the one classroom laptop and they do not? If yes, might you get over it by realizing that what is fair is that everyone gets what they need in order to learn?

EXAMPLE: We don't say one student cannot wear glasses or take his anti-seizure medicine only because it would not be fair to the rest of the students who are not given eyeglasses or anti-seizure medicine.

✓ Would you like some ideas on how to explain autism to the rest of the students, their parents and the staff at your school? If so, please see *Walk Awhile in My Autism* (McGinnity and Negri 2005).

Blue-Green Leaves Variables

Blue-Green Leaves
1st or 2nd
or 3rd?
Oh my!

Or maybe
4th or 5th?

How am I to know what is which
When eyes play tricks
And then sometimes

Oh, my!
My eyes
Beyond their tricks do take me

Way on over to
Reality's Variations

Disturbingly entrancing
Blue-Green Leaves enhancing

An experiential specialty
Of my very own neurology

Unfolding secret beauty
Unobserved by others

Which when
I try to tell them
Only gets me labeled

They do the best they can
But lack
In understanding

Experience of
Autistic
Brain-producing
Specialties

That I think of as blessings!

Shimmer Changed Leaves

Magnified Leaves

Olive-Green Leaves

An Aspect of My Autism

Oftentimes my autistic neurology delivers information in a way that cause objects to look different to me than those same objects might look to other people. The painting *Olive-Green Leaves* illustrates how an entire given scene (in this case of *Blue-Green Leaves* on pages 154 and 155) can become shades darker. This can happen when my sensory system is overloaded. In fact, for me, it is a reliable clue that downtime is needed when the bright blue-greens in the environment turn into the olive-green browns as illustrated in this painting.

At times my brain automatically picks out some minor detail, magnifying that one small piece of information (*Magnified Leaves*). When this happens I am left with only the magnified bit of the picture, having lost the whole. If I force myself to see the whole, I will lose the detail of the magnified bits. *Magnified Leaves* illustrates a bit from the whole of *Olive-Green Leaves*.

Other times my brain does what I call a shimmer change. During these times the object I am looking at becomes entranced in a shimmer that has the effect of duplicating aspects of the original image in a way that makes a shimmering movement. When this happens the shimmer color is different from the color of the original image. Typically, shimmer changes are quite beautiful. Even so, it becomes very difficult to know if I am looking at the same or a completely different image. *Shimmer Changed Leaves* is an example of this sort of change my brain could make when looking at any of the *Blue-Green Leaves* or at the *Olive-Green Leaves*.

Considerations When Working With Others

- At different times during my growing up, and even during my adult years, autism wasn't something people knew much about. I often came in front of mental health professionals. It is important to know that if you go to a mental health professional, or take your child to a mental health professional, in all probability you will walk out with a diagnosis of a mental condition as found in the *DSM-5*, otherwise known as the *Diagnostic and Statistical Manual of Mental Disorders* (2013) 5th ed.

In my adult life I obtained a master's degree in social work. I did clinical work diagnosing and treating people in psychiatric settings. Eventually, I limited my practice to autism. When I worked as a clinician, a diagnostic checklist was required for the patient. Even if I didn't know for sure if the patient met all the criteria, I would need to write a provisional or working diagnosis for the patient's medical records. This was necessary for the clinic to be able to receive reimbursement from the medical insurance company. Therefore, when a person receives services from a mental health clinic, that person will wind up with a mental health diagnosis. Whether they are told that diagnosis or not, it will be in their medical records.

I take the time to explain this because many times as a patient I have received mental health diagnoses that were not accurate, even though I met the criteria to receive each of the diagnoses at the time they were given. For example, as a teen I was asked if I saw things that other people don't see, if I saw things that really weren't there, if I heard voices that others don't hear, etc. The answers to all these questions were "yes."

Because of my autism neurology, even though I hadn't yet been diagnosed with autism, my sense of sight and sense of hearing delivered much more detailed information to me than was typically experienced by the majority of people. Moreover, that information, as illustrated by *Olive-Green Leaves, Magnified Leaves,* and *Shimmer Changed Leaves*, was sometimes skewed. This was a function of my autism neurology rather than indications of schizophrenia. Thus, treatment for schizophrenia was not at all successful (Endow 2009a).

- ✓ Have you or your child sought out the help of a mental health professional?

    If so, it may be wise to find out if the particular provider you see has experience working with people who have an autism neurology. This is because what can appear to be a psychiatric symptom can sometimes be more accurately described as a function of autistic thinking. The distinction is important because it drives treatment.

    EXAMPLE: Hallucinations need to be treated. Thinking in pictures does not.

- ✓ When a person with autism reports their experience, are you quick to negate it only because your own neurology informs you differently?

    You may not be able to share the experience of an autistic because your own neurology is set up differently, but that doesn't mean the autistic experience is any less real than your experience! It only means it is different.

EXAMPLE: Tywanika, a second-grader, was most upset because the swing she loved to use on the playground was shooting molten space daggers into her eyes. The swing only did this during afternoon recess. The swing did not shoot these molten space daggers during morning or lunch recess.

Both her teacher and her assistant assured Tywanika that molten space daggers were not real. They were trying to be helpful, but their words did not negate Tywanika's experience. It was more helpful to gather information from Tywanika about these molten space daggers, as she was well able to answer questions. She revealed that the molten space daggers lived in the swing chains and only speared her eyes in the afternoon.

What looked like a possible psychiatric problem turned out to be something much different! The molten space daggers phenomena first started on the Monday after the springtime change when clocks are moved ahead an hour. This made Tywanika's recess time coincide with the sun at a slightly different level in the sky. As the sunrays bounced off the metal chains of the swing, Tywanika's sensitive sensory system noticed the difference in a way to cause her experience to be that of molten space daggers being thrust into her eyes.

When Tywanika was taken out to the swings an hour earlier and an hour later in the afternoon the problem did not occur. Tywanika could then understand what was happening. It was only a few weeks until the sun had shifted enough that the bright reflection off the swing chains was no longer problematic.

- Sometimes I am told that a child with autism laughs when there is nothing to laugh about. This translates to mean that a child with autism laughs when there is nothing observable by an NT to laugh about. In my experience autistic students do not arbitrarily laugh at nothing for the sole purpose of disturbing their classmates!

As a child I often laughed out loud when I saw the sparkles from the fluorescent lights in my classroom swirl around with the shimmering lights shooting out from them as they moved. This happened when the classroom door was opened quickly or when a breeze came in through the window.

I still see the same phenomena today when I am in schools consulting, but I no longer laugh. I have learned along the way that others do not share my experience and when I laugh it seems out of context. In fact, it can disturb people when they do not share the context that generates my behavior. Thus, today I refrain from laughing at classroom shimmer lights when they occur.

- ✓ Do you find yourself saying your student laughs (or insert another behavior) for no reason? If yes, do you now know there very likely is a reason for the laughing (or other behavior) even if that reason is not apparent to your neurology?

- ✓ Will you now assume your student's behaviors are reasonable given his autism neurology?

    This does not mean you cannot work with your student to trade-in behaviors that don't work for behaviors that work better in the classroom while meeting the original function of the behavior.

- ✓ Will you please stop attributing negative intentionality to autistics when you cannot ascertain a reason for a behavior you perceive as annoying?

    Instead, adopt positive regard for a person with a neurology different from yours and work with that person toward a more positive outcome for all.

Fractured Vision

Five years old
Across the street
I see

Some clouds
A boy
Some sky
Two birds
No…it's three

And four trees
No…one tree
Oh, my, a topless one!

Some shoes
Some grass
Some sun
I see

Separate parts
Unconnected pieces

Of
An unknown whole

Is what
Fractured Vision
Delivered to me.

Fifty years later
I paint
These pieces

Of
Across the street.

Oh, my!
I discover
Kite Boy—

That's
What I
Was seeing!

Kite Boy

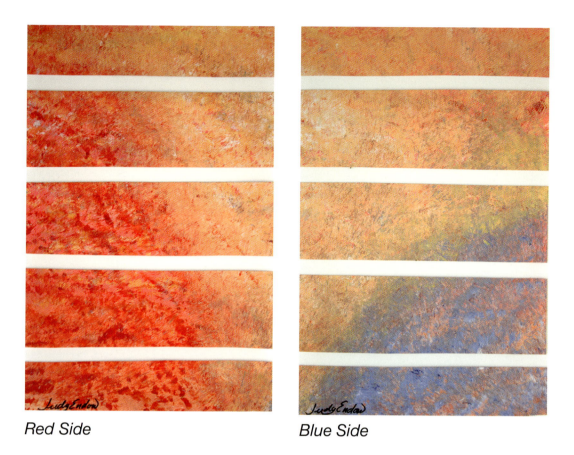

Red Side *Blue Side*

Blue Mountain

Blue Mountain Panorama

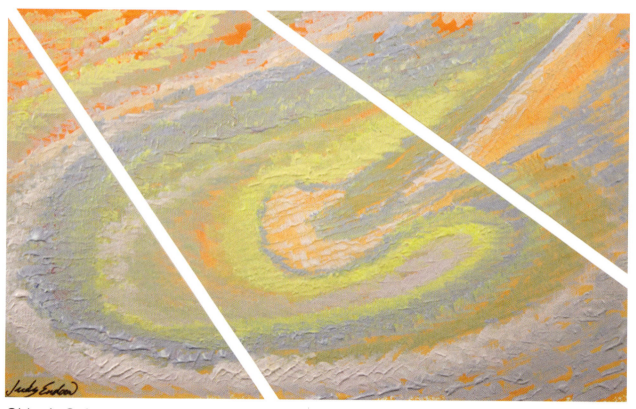
Chloe's Colors

First Painting

An Aspect of My Autism

These paintings (*Kite Boy, Blue Mountain Panorama, Red Side, Blue Side, Chloe's Colors,* and *First Painting*) illustrate what I call fractured vision. Sometimes my autistic neurology delivers images I see as if they were cut into pieces. Most often these "fractures" occur along straight lines, but sometimes the "fractures" cause what I am looking at to appear so jumbled that it is difficult to make sense of what I am seeing. When I look at a fractured piece of the image, I lose the big picture context of the whole. When I look at the whole, I am unable to distinguish the pieces. This way of seeing things is not constant. Thus, I can perform a skill one day and not the next. This fractured vision happens most often when I am in sensory overload.

Considerations When Working With Others

- Many times students with autism are able to perform a skill one day and then not the next. It is frustrating for teachers and for parents. Imagine how frustrating it is for the autistic! There are many possible reasons for this variable performance. Indeed, some of the reasons may not yet be known! The take-away point here is that regardless of whether we know or understand the reason for variable performance, when autism neurology is involved—there IS a reason!

    ✓ Do you side with or against your student when he is unable to perform a previously mastered skill?

    EXAMPLE: When your student stands at the bottom of the stairwell without attempting to climb the stairs when he has previously climbed these same stairs many times do you

    a.) assume intentionality and attribute a negative character trait such as stubborn, obstinate or refusing;

    OR

    b.) assume his autism is giving him a hard time?

    ✓ Your assumption about the student is important because it determines your response. Will you

    a.) try to cajole, embarrass or make a negative example of your student in hopes of motivating him to climb the stairs you know he can climb;

> OR
>
> b.) will you say something like, "It looks like your autism is giving you a hard time?"

- I am explaining my experience of the way autism visits my body not to cause you to think that autism visits every autistic in this way, but instead for you to know that autistic neurology often changes up the way the world is perceived and experienced. I do not like it when I want to do one thing and my body does not cooperate. It is very frustrating when my body betrays me. It only makes the problematic situation worse when others ascribe intentionality or assume negative character traits. I know if you were doing what I am doing in these situations, you would be willfully employing the behavior (or lack of behavior). However, because of our different neurologies, our identical actions do not have a shared meaning.

    - ✓ Do my explanations cause you to wonder and perhaps to reconsider some of the ways you think when it comes to attributing intentionality to autistics who may act in ways that are out of the range of what is generally considered typical? (I hope so!)

    - ✓ Even if you are unsure, will you assume the best of your student with autism?

        Ask yourself what might be the outcome of assuming the best versus assuming negative intentionality of your student when he does not perform a skill previously mastered?

        What if you are right?

        What if you are wrong?

        If you truly are still not convinced and need to make some sort of assumption, what is the least dangerous assumption (Leary and Donnellan 2012)?

Living

Chapter Seven: Engaging

Brown Paper Bags

Perhaps a bit scruffy
Perhaps with some tears
Perhaps even with
The bottom missing

Is My rendering
Of
Today's Brown Paper Bag autistics

Autistics...
Often defined
By the world
As
A lump generic commodity
Of what's missing
As measured
By NT society norms
Dictated by WHO IS
Otherwise known as John Q. Public

So
Brown Paper Bags
I sculptured ceramically
To stand sturdily
Marking our today-place
In history

A declaration to all
Of
Autistic beauty
Uniqueness
And blessing

Perhaps one day
John Q. Public
Will purchase his ticket for travel

To see
The Brown Paper Bags
WE ALREADY ARE
Despite concurrently awaiting discovery
By
Much of
Society's Tomorrow

Brown Paper Bag A1

Brown Paper Bag A4

Brown Bag A3

An Aspect of My Autism

For most of my life I have been a stranger to myself, not really understanding who I am as a person. This is because I have always been measured according to how far I deviated from the normal majority of people. It took me until I was in my fifties to realize that I am a person in my own right. I am not simply the sum total of my measure of deviation from the norm.

I have had a hard time understanding myself as a person because nobody ever really looked at what made me be me in this world. Instead, I have only been measured by what I am not—my absence of NT-ness so to speak. It hasn't been until very recently that I have discovered other autistics and have come to realize that our way of being in the world is valid. Even though it is different, the autistic way of being is just as valid as the neurotypical way of being. I am just as much a human being as anyone else!

Now that I understand I am a valid human being, I no longer define myself in the way society defines me in terms of what I am not. I now think of myself in terms of who and what I am, rather than as a less-than human being with missing characteristics or less-than attributes. This has been a powerful difference that has changed my outlook on life. If you read my older books (Endow 2006; Endow 2009a) you will see the difference from the way I thought even a few years ago!

Considerations When Working With Others

- All children need to know who they are rather than who they are not. It is difficult for autistic children to learn who they are when they are only defined in terms of who and what they are not according to the degree of deviation from the neurotypical normal of other children.

This is NOT a case against using deficit-based language as a measure of diagnosis and a reason for intervention. This IS a case against using deficit-based language to define the humanity of autistics. There is a subtle, yet monumental and powerful difference.

✓ Do you think about your student only in terms of his deviation from NT standards?

✓ Do you think about your student only in terms of how he is different from other students?

- ✓ Do you think about your student only in light of your understanding of autism?

- ✓ Do you know HOW your student experiences the world, HOW he experiences other people, and HOW he experiences everyday events?

  Or do you only know that he does not experience things the same way as most students?

- ✓ Do you have a way to identify and learn about the positive qualities of autistics that typical people do not possess?

The Essence of People

Melodious sounds
From your
Colors

Are music
To my ears

Or not

The patterns
Of swirls
Of the colors
Of you
Emanate
From your being

When matches
I make
I can
Conversate

We connect

My soul
With yours
Beyond words

But if not
Then
I can't

Leaving
You to be you
And
Me to be me

Each
In
The essence
Of
Our
Being

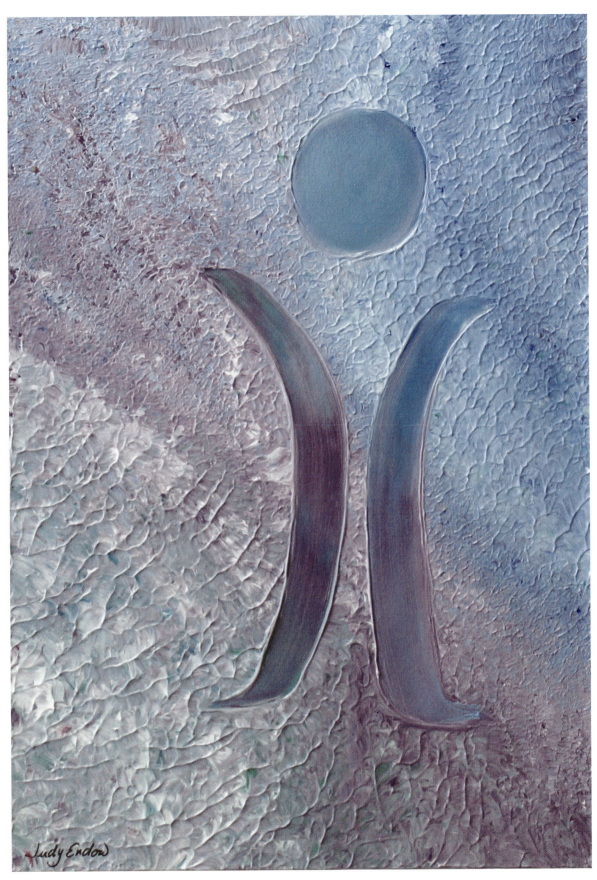

Blue-Lavender People

Green People on Pink

Pink-Orange People Pair

Sunshine People

Autumn Water People

An Aspect of My Autism

I rarely remember the same details about other people that most folks do. I remember the visual perception that came to me during an interaction, whether or not I was personally a part of that interaction. I pick up much information through seeing the sounds and movements of color people generate and changes in the air space surrounding them as they speak and go about their business. When I match the colors of others I can carry on a conversation. When our colors don't match, the conversation usually doesn't go well. I did not realize this way of perceiving and understanding the essence of people is not shared by others until recent years.

Considerations When Working With Others

- My autistic neurology means that I am not good at picking up social cues, understanding complex social situations, automatically picking up meanings of idioms, or understanding the hidden curriculum that most others automatically pick up (Endow 2012). This means I often look naïve and gullible. The fact is I AM naïve and gullible when I try to use the social constructs of neurotypicals to navigate the world around me.

The above two paragraphs are important to put together. Together they mean that while I have great difficulty operating as an NT in the world, I am an expert at operating in my own way. This means when I follow my own ways I can figure out which people to interact with and which ones to avoid. I can know who is out to do harm and who isn't. I can know who does not have my interests at heart and who does. This is important because it allows me to navigate everyday life avoiding personal harm and gathering good people around me EVEN THOUGH my social skills and abilities are not those of typical people.

When others try to help me they most often try to get me to understand the world in the way they understand the world. This is very helpful in allowing me to understand how typical people might talk and act. However, it works best when I can understand the ways of typical people while at the same time honoring my own neurology. In fact, even though I can learn how typical people think about something, it does not help me to be able to think in their way. It is similar to the fact that just because I explained my visual way of thinking, incorporating the sound and movement of colors, does not mean that now you understand how I think and that now you can think the way I think! We think differently and that is okay.

This means I may avoid business interactions with someone because they have ugly colors with sticky tentacles moving sneakily toward me. A typical person may understand that this potential business partner is devious and less than ethical in his practices. It is good for me to understand how to ferret out devious and unethical intentions because it helps me to intellectually understand why I am not engaging in business with the person. However, this is not in accordance with my first language. It is not how I innately understand people. Just like it would not be helpful for you to adopt my ways which are foreign to you, please understand that it is not helpful for me to always adopt your foreign ways when making decisions about people.

- ✓ Do you know how your autistic child remembers people?
- ✓ Do you know what is important to your autistic child about other people?
- ✓ Do you understand how your child with autism decides who to interact with and who not to interact with?
- ✓ Do you honor this, even if you may not understand it?

3 Panel People

Green
Swirls
With blue
Drawing in
White too

Melodious
Sitting-still-white
Sings
To the green
And
The blue

Then blue
Reaches
Out
Subliminally composing
Variegated
Melodies for taking

While green
Mixes
Together
White-chosen songs
With
The dance of the blue

A drama
Of
Work unfolding
Through the
Sharing
Of
Personal essence

By
The green
And the white
And the blue

3 Panel People

An Aspect of My Autism

People often assume that I do not like to be social. I think this happens because the way I am social looks different from the way typical people are social. I very much enjoy being in the presence of others at social gatherings. I like to watch people as they talk with one another. I love seeing all the swirls of the sounds and movements of the colors of these interactions. I am not so good at paying attention to the particular words people say or in responding to them quickly in a conversation. Because I do not engage in group conversations in the way most people do, it is often assumed that I do not like to be social.

It is true that I do not like many aspects that seem to be part of the context of social events, but only because they are difficult for my sensory system to handle when grouped together. Social events typically will have loud music, eating and drinking and movement of people. This is in addition to the main activity or reason for the event such as a birthday party, sports game, picnic, etc. Many times there are strange lighting effects and a myriad of clashing smells of people's various scents (natural and chemical) along with the variety of food and drinks being served. Adding all these elements to talking with people makes it very difficult for me. Even so, the conclusion that I do not like being social is incorrect. Let's just say it is difficult for me to enjoy social activity in this sort of context.

I do love being in the presence of people when they are engaged in an activity or simply in conversation (*3 Panel People*). When I don't have to reciprocate in like manner with others, but can instead simply be there and say something only occasionally—that is the best! Without the expectation that I will talk just as much as the rest of the people, I am able to be relaxed and enjoy the other people by watching them interact. I can hear their words and allow my natural way of processing to occur.

When I am expected to respond in the typical timing of social conversation, it means that I can never totally process what other people are saying before I need to say something back. When I am unable to incorporate what others are saying in my responding, they wind up thinking that either I am not intelligent enough to understand what they are saying, or that I only want to talk about my interests and not their interests. While I can understand why they might think this way, their assumptions about me are incorrect.

Considerations When Working With Others

- When people have autism, by definition they deviate from the norm in social and communication abilities as displayed by neurotypical people. It is also quite common for them to have sensory differences as compared to NTs. It is amazing to me how often these three most difficult parts of my autism are all rolled into one event that is labeled a social occasion, and then people wonder why it is difficult for me. Moreover, based on the fact that it IS difficult for me, they assume that I do not like to be social. The truth is I enjoy many aspects of social events, but not all at the same time!

- ✓ When your child appears uncomfortable at social events do you assume he does not like to be social?

- ✓ Does your child enjoy specific elements of a social event when the element is isolated from the context of the myriad of factors that happen all together to create the experience of a social event?

- ✓ How does it work well for your child to be in the company of other people?

- ✓ Will you create opportunities for your child to be social on terms that are comfortable and meaningful to him?

- Remember that autism is measured by absence of neurotypicality. Also, please know that not having skills or abilities in an area does not mean I dislike it. For example, because I don't measure up to NT standards in social skills does not mean that I dislike being social. Because I do not measure up to NT standards in conversational abilities does not mean that I do not like to talk to people. Because I do not measure up to NT standards in my ability to tolerate the sensory bombardment that happens at a birthday party does not mean that I do not like birthday parties. It serves me best to figure out how I can do what I like even though it is difficult for me. Please don't let my measure of absence of neurotypicality allow me to be defined as a NOT-real-person sort of being.

  - ✓ Do you define your child by the absence of neurotypicality rather than by the presence of who he is and what he can do?

  - ✓ Do you assume your child does not like to be social because it is difficult for him to negotiate the context of social occasions?

  - ✓ How does your child enjoy meeting his social needs? (Please keep in mind that all human beings, including your child, have social needs.)

Connections

Out of sight
Means
Out of mind

Unless

A
Picture
I
Create

Before
I
Knew
To
Do
This

A
Friend
I
Had no way
To
Keep

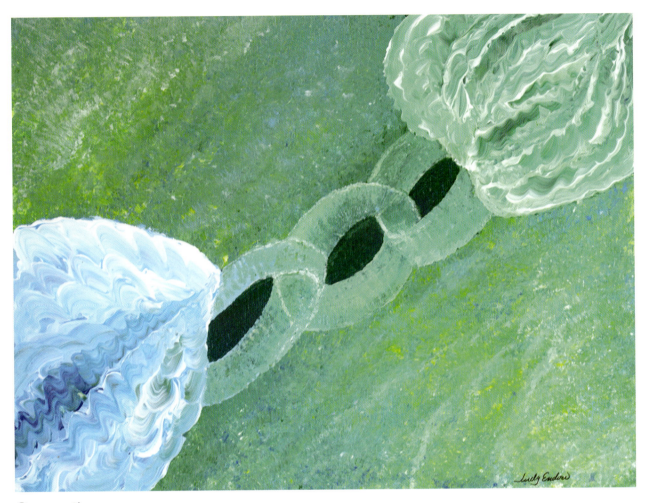

Connections

Whispering Strength A1

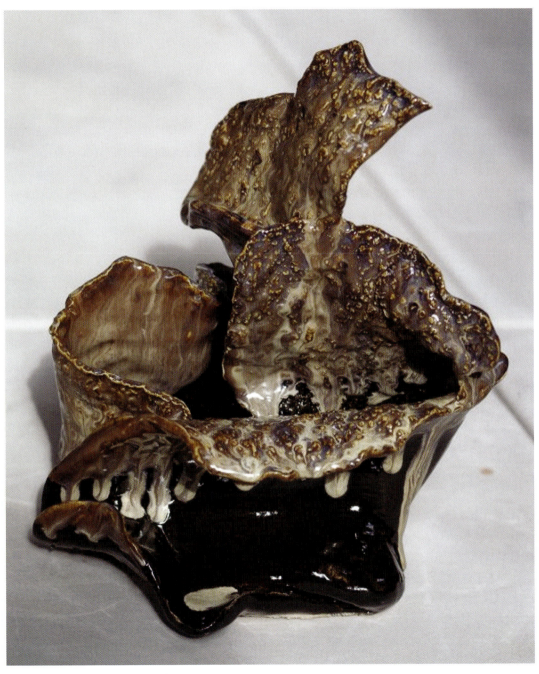

Whispering Strength A2

An Aspect of My Autism

My connections to other people are perceived visually. In fact, I often need to have a concrete visual to enable me to think of my friends or to even know where they are if they travel often. One friend sends me links to hotels where she will be staying. When I go to the link I can find enough of a visual to allow me to stay connected to my friend even though she is in another state or another country.

Another friend has her administrative assistant send me her travel itinerary. This printed itinerary becomes a visual that allows me to remain connected over time and space. The funny thing about this is that in the beginning I needed to print off the schedule each month. Over time, just knowing it was on my computer and I could print it off if I needed was enough. Today I no longer get this friend's monthly travel itinerary, but instead have painted a picture that now serves as my visual connection of our friendship (*Connections*).

Sometimes I need an actual physical visual to understand my relationship to another person and at other times I am able to pop up a visual in my head. Regardless of how or where I get my visual, the fact remains that I need some sort of visual in order to experience the fact that I am connected to another person through the bond of friendship (*Whispering Strength* series). This doesn't make sense to most people, but I have learned not to let that bother me these days! I do what makes sense to my neurology to maintain and participate in friendships. My closest friends tend to be people who do not question this peculiarity but instead join with me in honoring it.

Considerations When Working With Others

- Children with autism may need a visual placeholder for a person when that person is not present. This placeholder may need to be an actual picture of the person. Sometimes it can be something that reminds the child of the person. The reason for this is because when a child is a visual thinker and has not yet learned to create a picture/visual to represent people, he has no way to think about a person when he cannot see them. This means out of sight, out of mind. It seems to be difficult to get NTs to understand this phenomenon, but when this happens it is as if the out of sight person is no longer alive. A child may grieve as if his mother has died when he has no way to create or hold a picture of his mother in his mind when they are separated.

- ✓ Does your child need a picture of people important to him when those people are not physically present?

- ✓ Might your child benefit if he were to develop a way to create an internal picture of people who are important to him?

- ✓ If your child has difficulty when separated from a significant person might it be helpful for him to have a picture of that person or something that reminds him of that person?

- Many autistics are visual thinkers. It is no wonder visuals also play an important part in developing and maintaining relationships! Many autistics need something they can actually see to remind and assure them that a bond of friendship exists. Oftentimes if we make this need known we are laughed at or in some other way ridiculed. It is thought to be babyish and we are admonished to "grow up."

I do not understand this reaction of others, but have experienced it many times over the years. It is not at all helpful. It does not honor my neurology and it does not allow me to participate in relationships. It seems to be difficult for NTs to imagine relationship connections to be any way other than the way that works for them—which does not typically include a picture or object reminder of a friend in order to maintain the bond of connection.

- ✓ Do you poke fun at those things in your child that are different or that you do not understand?

- ✓ Do you allow others to tease your child, hoping that the teasing will encourage him to be more like NTs?

- ✓ Do you honor and support your child's neurology even when it means you will be misunderstood as a parent or your parenting skills will become frowned upon?

- ✓ Do you support relationships your child has with others in a way that make sense to him, even though it may not make sense to you?

Living

Chapter Eight: Conclusion

In Sidewalk Cracks

In life we play on sidewalk squares.
You on your NT sidewalk square
Me, on my autistic one.

You jump to my square to help me out
Because
Heaven knows
(and so does everyone else)
That I need all the help you can give.

You teach me to copy your ways.
I learn to do so.
I jump to your square and copy you.

You are happy because I am learning
To look like you
To copy your ways in the world.

I am empty.
All I have is you helping me
And me copying your ways.
Is it a wonder the feeling of alien predominates?

There is more to jumping over the sidewalk crack.

Instead, let's jump in it!
You from your square
And me from mine
Together jumping into the crack between

A real relationship in the making
Not you helping
Not me copying
But instead
Both together

Each ourselves
And together
Friends being!

In Sidewalk Cracks 5

In Sidewalk Cracks 1

In Sidewalk Cracks 2

I have come to understand relationships by looking at sidewalks. I imagine people each on their own sidewalk square. Growing up I had many helpers. People who were helpers would jump from their own sidewalk square over to my sidewalk square. They would stand by me on my sidewalk square and help me. Eventually, I came to learn their ways.

Once I learned to copy the ways of other people, I was allowed to jump over to their sidewalk square and occupy space with them. This jumping around on sidewalk squares happened in various ways for most of my life. It wasn't very fulfilling. I often felt like an alien, other-ed, sometimes allowed and always oddly different.

Then I learned something new! I learned about jumping into the sidewalk crack with another human being. I discovered that in sidewalk cracks is the place of real relationship. It is the place where we each come as we are and it is perfectly fine. We are at home with each other in this space regardless of which version of self we bring that day. As we jump from our square into this sidewalk crack we find that together we are more than the sum of our individual parts and we find that each is necessary to the other. It is a relationship of equality based on our separate commodities of uniqueness.

In conclusion, I want you, the reader, to know I have come to learn that even though I do not measure up to be very many inches when the yardstick of NT normal is used (Endow 2009a), I no longer use these very little bit of inches to define my human worth. Instead, I count all of my inches that nobody has yet found a way to measure. I have used painting and sculpture to offer you a glimpse into how my autistic neurology allows me to perceive the world around me. In the process of sharing with you I have come up strong and tall. I grew tall, rising up out of the sidewalk cracks of meaningful friendships. I grew strong in the sharing with you by deciding to count the inches of my tallness that the NT yardstick cannot yet measure. I am blessed.
My heart is full. I have you, the reader to thank. If you are still reading, thank you for walking this journey with me. I appreciate you!

Epilogue

Through sharing my art and my words, specifics of some of my experiences of the world in the way my autism neurology makes information available to me have been illustrated. While you may find it interesting, it is important to remind yourself that each person with autism experiences his or her autism in a unique way. While another autistic may not share my exact experience of autism, please allow my experience to cause you to pause…

Yes,
Please pause
And
Wonder

How does my child with autism experience the world?

Look for the beauty.
Watch for the challenges.

Take pleasure in the magnificence.
Your child's way of experiencing the world is that one-in-a-million we all treasure.

Outsmart the challenges.
Life can be hard.
Make love stronger.

Never give up.
Keep on keeping on.

Know you do not walk alone.
Many have traveled down your same road.

A legacy has been left for you.
What legacy will you leave for those coming down your path
Tomorrow?

In the meantime, here is my experience for you for today.
Please see the beauty in the hard of my autism.

And be encouraged
Is my wish for you.

Sincerely,
Judy

References

American Psychiatric Association. 2013. *Diagnostic and Statistical Manual of Mental Disorders* (5th ed.). Washington, DC: Author.

Åsberg, J., S. O. Dahlgren, and A. Dahlgren Sandberg. 2008. Basic reading skills in high-functioning Swedish children with autism spectrum disorders or attention disorder. *Research in Autism Spectrum Disorders 2* (1): 95-109.

Åsberg, J., S. Kopp, K. Berg-Kelly, and C. Gilberg. 2010. Reading comprehension, word decoding and spelling in girls with autism spectrum disorders (ASD) or attention-deficit/hyperactivity disorders (AD/HD): performance and predictors. *International Journal of Language and Communication Disorders* 45: 61-71.

Buron, K. D., and P. Wolfberg. 2008. *Learners on the Autism Spectrum: Preparing highly qualified educators*. Overland Park, KS: AAPC Publishing.

Endow, J. 2006. *Making Lemonade: Hints for autism's helpers*. Cambridge, WI: Cambridge Book Review Press.

Endow, J. 2009a. *Paper Words: Discovering and living with my autism*. Shawnee Mission, KS: AAPC Publishing.

Endow, J. 2009b. *The Power of Words: How we talk about people with autism spectrum disorders matters!* DVD. Shawnee Mission, KS: AAPC Publishing.

Endow, J. 2011. *Practical Solutions for Stabilizing Students With Classic Autism to Be Ready to Learn: Getting to go*. Shawnee Mission, KS: AAPC Publishing.

Endow, J. 2012. *Learning the Hidden Curriculum: The odyssey of one autistic adult*. Shawnee Mission, KS: AAPC Publishing.

Leary, M. R., and A. M. Donnellan. 2012. *Autism: Sensory-movement differences and diversity*. Cambridge, WI: Cambridge Book Review Press.

Minshew, N. J., G. Goldstein, H. G. Taylor, D. J. Siegel. 1994. Academic achievement in high functioning autistic individuals. *Journal of Clinical and Experimental Neuropsychology* 16: 261-270.

Myles, B. S., T. D. Hilgenfeld, G. P. Barnhill, D. E. Griswold, T. Hagiwara, and R. L. Simpson. 2002. Analysis of reading skills in individuals with Asperger Syndrome. *Focus on Autism and Other Developmental Disabilities* 17 (1): 44-47.

Myles, B. S., J. Endow, and M. Mayfield. 2013. *The Hidden Curriculum of Getting and Keeping a Job: Navigating the social landscape of employment; A guide for individuals with autism spectrum and other social-cognitive challenges*. Shawnee Mission, KS: AAPC Publishing.

Nation, K., P. Clarke, B. J. Wright, and C. Williams. 2006. Patterns of reading ability in children with autism spectrum disorders. *Journal of Autism and Developmental Disorders* 36: 911-919.

Negri, N., and K. McGinnity. 2005. *Walk Awhile in My Autism*. Cambridge, WI: Cambridge Book Review Press.

Newman, T. M., D. Macomber, A. J. Naples, T. Babitz, F. Volkmar, and E. L. Grigorenko. 2007. Hyperlexia in children with autism spectrum disorder. *Journal of Autism and Developmental Disorders* 37: 760-774.

Robledo, J. A., and A. M. Donnellan. 2008. Properties of supportive relationships from the perspective of academically successful individuals with autism. *Intellectual Developmental Disabilities* 46 (4): 299-310.

Snow, K. "People First Language." http://www.disabilityisnatural.com/explore/people-first-language. Website accessed 2013.

Williams, D. "Autism and Dissociative Disorders." http://www.donnawilliams.net/333.0.html. Website accessed 2013.

Artwork Chapter Index

Dedication
1. *Lavender Flower*, 7

Chapter One
2. *Sun Waves*, 21
3. *Right Sun*, 22
4. *Left Sun*, 23
5. *Predawn Tail*, 26
6. *Morning Tail*, 27
7. *Wide Tail*, 28
8. *Earth Tail*, 29
9. *Earth-Tail Pink*, 30
10. *Earth-Tail Purple*, 31
11. *Water-Tail Pink*, 32
12. *Water-Tail Purple*, 33

Chapter Two
13. *Summer-Tail Mist*, 38
14. *Fall-Tail Mist*, 39
15. *SNOW-Tail Mist*, 41
16. *LAKE-Tail Mist*, 42
17. *EARTH-Tail Mist*, 43
18. *Morning-Chirp Sun Girl*, 46
19. *Night-Song Sun Girl*, 47
20. *Cloud-Breath Sun Girl*, 47
21. *Moon Sparkle Winter*, 48
22. *Moon Sparkle Spring*, 49
23. *Moon Sparkle Summer*, 50
24. *Moon Sparkle Fall*, 51

Chapter Three
25. *Sky Glory Blue*, 59
26. *Sky Glory Diamonds*, 60
27. *Sky Glory Day*, 62
28. *Sky Glory Moon*, 63
29. *One Person Tail*, 67
30. *One Person Tail Intrusion*, 68
31. *Two Person Tail Intrusion*, 69
32. *Diminished Sun 1*, 71
33. *Diminished Sun 2*, 72
34. *Diminished Sun 3*, 73

Chapter Four
35. *Heartbreak Night Tail*, 80
36. *Heartbreak Day Tail*, 81
37. *Look Me In the Eye*, 86
38. *Buzzing Bones*, 87
39. *Eye Fish*, 88
40. *SIZZLE POP*, 89
41. *Eye Trees*, 90
42. *Eye Land*, 91
43. *STRIKE ME*, 92
44. *Eye Tulip*, 93
45. *Goldenrod 2*, 95
46. *Goldenrod 3*, 96
47. *Goldenrod 4*, 97
48. *Snow Melting*, 100
49. *Spring Hill*, 101
50. *AIRSCAPE*, 103
51. *GROUNDSCAPE*, 104
52. *PICTURE TREE*, 105
53. *Goodness Bay*, 107
54. *Goodness Hills*, 108
55. *Goodness Tree*, 109
56. *Dawn Inclusion Making*, 115
57. *Twilight Inclusion Making*, 116
58. *Dusk Inclusion Making*, 117
59. *Girl on Dock*, 119

Chapter Five

60. *Arctic Waves*, 129
61. *Lavender-Tan Wave*, 129
62. *Orange Wave*, 130
63. *Orange-Pink White Wave*, 131
64. *Bright Surf*, 132
65. *Hawaii Surf*, 133
66. *Planetary Sky Upper Left*, 138
67. *Planetary Sky Lower Left*, 138
68. *Planetary Sky Upper Right*, 139
69. *Planetary Sky Lower Right*, 139
70. *White Thought Wave on Earth-Fire*, 145
71. *Lavender Thought Wave on Green*, 146
72. *White-Pink Thought Wave on Orange*, 146
73. *White Thought Wave on Lavender Blues*, 147
74. *White Thought Wave on Green*, 147

Chapter Six

75. *5th Blue-Green Leaves*, 153
76. *1st Blue-Green Leaves*, 154
77. *3rd Blue-Green Leaves*, 154
78. *2nd Blue-Green Leaves*, 155
79. *4th Blue-Green-Leaves*, 155
80. *Shimmer Changed Leaves*, 161
81. *Magnified Leaves*, 162
82. *Olive-Green Leaves*, 163
83. *Kite Boy*, 169
84. *Red Side*, 170
85. *Blue Side*, 170
86. *Blue Mountain*, 170
87. *Blue Mountain Panorama*, 171
88. *Chloe's Colors*, 172
89. *First Painting*, 173

Chapter Seven

90. *Brown Paper Bag A1*, 179
91. *Brown Paper Bag A4*, 180
92. *Brown Paper Bag A3*, 181
93. *Blue-Lavender People*, 185
94. *Green People on Pink*, 186
95. *Pink-Orange People Pair*, 187
96. *Sunshine People*, 188
97. *Autumn Water People*, 189
98. *3 Panel People*, 193
99. *Connections*, 197
100. *Whispering Strength A1*, 198
101. *Whispering Strength A2*, 199

Chapter Eight

102. *In Sidewalk Cracks 5*, 205
103. *In Sidewalk Cracks 1*, 206
104. *In Sidewalk Cracks 2*, 207

Photo Credits

Mark Dilley: 7, 129 [top], 130, 131, 132, 138, 139, 146, 147, 153, 154, 155, 161, 162, 163, 169, 170, 171, 172, 173, 186, 187, 188, 197

Judy Endow: 21, 22, 23, 26, 27, 28, 29, 30, 31, 32, 33, 38, 39, 41, 42, 43, 46, 47, 48, 49, 50, 51, 59, 60, 62, 63, 67, 68, 69, 71, 72, 73, 80, 81, 86, 87, 88, 89, 90, 91, 92, 93, 95, 96, 97, 100, 101, 103, 104, 105, 107, 108, 109, 115, 116, 117, 119, 129 [bottom], 133, 145, 181, 185, 189, 193, 205, 206, 207

Darren Hauck: 179, 180, 181, 198, 199